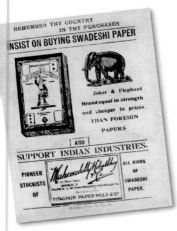

REMEMBER THY COUNTRY
IN THY PURCHASES
INSIST ON BUYING SWADESHI PAPER

Poster carrying an appeal
to buy Indian paper, 1940

EYEWITNESS
GANDHI

Bowl and plate
used by Gandhi

Written by
JUHI SAKLANI

Consultant
VIVEK BHANDARI

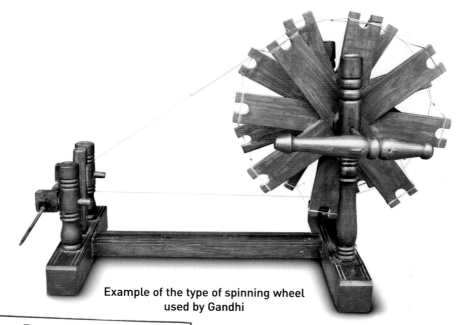

Example of the type of spinning wheel
used by Gandhi

Raw indigo dye
extracted from
Indigofera tinctoria plant

LONDON, NEW YORK,
MELBOURNE, MUNICH, and DELHI

Senior editor Dipali Singh
Editor Medha Gupta
Designers Astha Singh, Sukriti Sobti
Picture researcher Sakshi Saluja
Picture research manager Taiyaba Khatoon
Senior cartographer Swati Handoo
Cartography manager Suresh Kumar
Managing editor Alka Ranjan
Managing art editor Romi Chakraborty
DTP designers Nandkishor Acharya,
Ganesh Sharma, Jagtar Singh
Senior producer Charlotte Cade
Print programme manager Luca Frassinetti
Managing director Aparna Sharma

First published in India in 2014
This edition published in Great Britain
by Dorling Kindersley Limited,
80 Strand, London WC2R 0RL

Copyright © 2014 Dorling Kindersley Limited
A Penguin Random House Company

2 4 6 8 10 9 7 5 3 1

270659 – 07/14

A CIP catalogue record for this book is
available from the British Library.

ISBN: 978-1-4093-7058-1

Printed and bound in China by
South China Printing Co. Ltd

Discover more at
www.dk.com

Sign on the house in which
Gandhi lived in London

World Peace gong,
Gandhi Smriti, New Delhi

Sri Mahadevar
Temple, Vaikom,
Kerala

World War II poster showing an
Indian soldier in the British army

Replicas of the type of *khadau*
(wooden sandals) worn by Gandhi

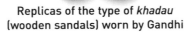

Gandhi in
Noakhali, East
Bengal (now in
Bangladesh)

EYEWITNESS

GANDHI

Includes poster

Indian caste pyramid

Examples of Gandhi's nature cure remedies

Replica of the cauldron in which Indians in South Africa burned passes in Hamidia Mosque, Johannesburg, in 1908

Prayer beads

Gandhi's spectacles

Gandhi's autobiography, *The Story of My Experiments with Truth*

Barrister Gandhi in London

Boer War medal

Coat of arms of the English East India Company

Gandhi Memorial in Gandhi Smriti, New Delhi

Three wise monkeys, epitomizing Gandhi's ideals

Contents

Example of the type of portable *charkha* used by Gandhi

Introducing Gandhi

Mohandas Karamchand Gandhi (2 October 1869–30 January 1948) was the inspirational political leader who led India to freedom from British colonial rule by adopting peaceful means of protest. Gandhi's commitment to the welfare of the poor, his efforts to bring harmony at all levels of society, and his personal asceticism earned him the epithet "Mahatma", or "great soul".

Coat of arms of Porbandar state

Product of his times

Gandhi was born in British India at a time when Indians were considered inferior. Even his father, a minister in the princely state of Porbandar, did not get the respect he deserved. Gandhi was also aware of the problems within his own society, such as discrimination against people from "lower castes" (*see* p.27).

"My life is my message."

MAHATMA GANDHI

Three wise monkeys

Covering their eyes, ears, and mouth with their hands, the three wise monkeys "see no evil, hear no evil, and speak no evil", epitomizing Gandhi's philosophy of truth and non-violence. Gifted to Gandhi by visitors from China, these monkeys fitted well with his idea of a truthful life.

Man of few possessions

The Mahatma was a deeply spiritual man who did not get distracted by worldly possessions or power. Identifying with India's poor, he lived very simply and only wore hand-woven *dhoti*, or loincloth. His pair of spectacles, pen, prayer book, spinning wheel, and wooden sandals were among his few personal belongings.

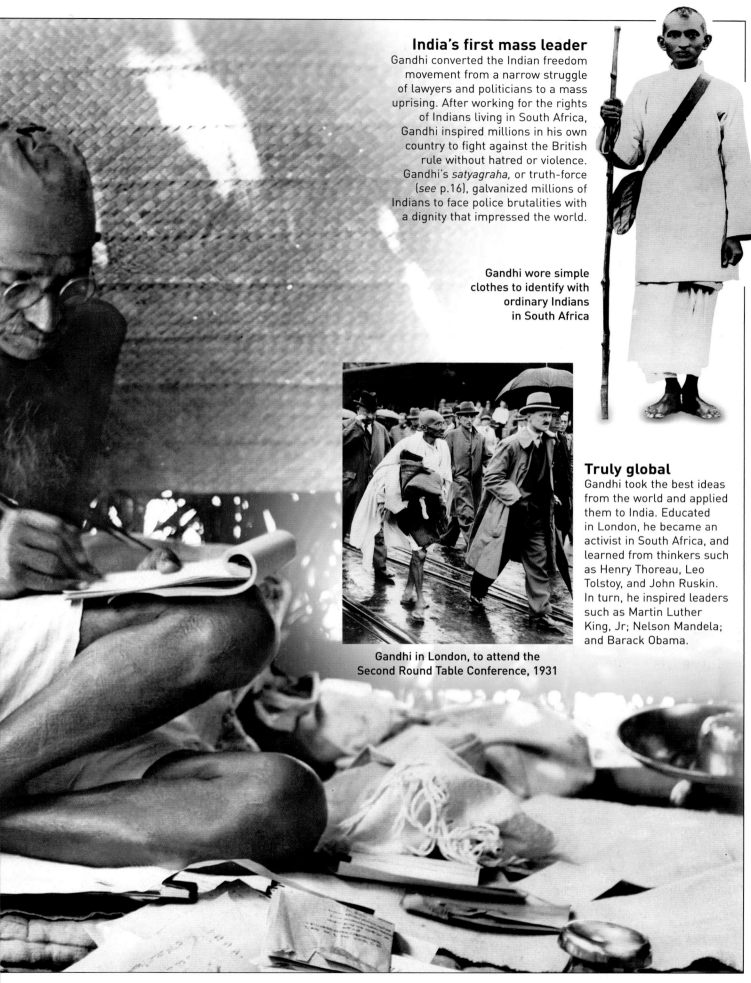

India's first mass leader

Gandhi converted the Indian freedom movement from a narrow struggle of lawyers and politicians to a mass uprising. After working for the rights of Indians living in South Africa, Gandhi inspired millions in his own country to fight against the British rule without hatred or violence. Gandhi's *satyagraha*, or truth-force (*see* p.16), galvanized millions of Indians to face police brutalities with a dignity that impressed the world.

Gandhi wore simple clothes to identify with ordinary Indians in South Africa

Gandhi in London, to attend the Second Round Table Conference, 1931

Truly global

Gandhi took the best ideas from the world and applied them to India. Educated in London, he became an activist in South Africa, and learned from thinkers such as Henry Thoreau, Leo Tolstoy, and John Ruskin. In turn, he inspired leaders such as Martin Luther King, Jr; Nelson Mandela; and Barack Obama.

British Empire

From the 15th to the 18th century, Europeans explored the world by sea in search of new trade routes. Countries such as Portugal, Spain, Britain, and France conquered territories and established colonies in the Americas, Africa, Asia, and Australia, bringing much of the world under their rule. Britain soon asserted its dominance with its superior gunpower, strong navy, and diplomacy, and created the mighty British Empire.

NORTH
AMERICA

PACIFIC
OCEAN

Trading empires

Between the late 15th and 18th centuries, the Portuguese and Dutch, followed by the British, developed large trading empires stretching to Africa, Asia, the Americas, and Australia. By the 17th century, the English East India Company, a merchant company, had gained a foothold in India by establishing Fort St George (in southern India) – an important port and entry point to India.

Industrial Revolution

Abundant raw material, available capital, and key technological developments, such as the steam engine, made conditions ripe for an industrial revolution in Britain. Invented by Thomas Newcomen in 1712, the steam engine was improved by James Watt. It replaced the water wheel and horses – which were slow and unreliable – as the main source of power for British industry, contributing to large-scale production and faster transportation by steamships and railways.

Slave
chains

Slave trade

Flexible ways of financing sea voyages lent fresh impetus to Britain's slave trade. By the 1780s, British ships were carrying 40,000 slaves from Africa to America annually. Trinkets, textiles, and weapons were sent to Africa and exchanged for slaves, who were sold for huge profit in the Americas.

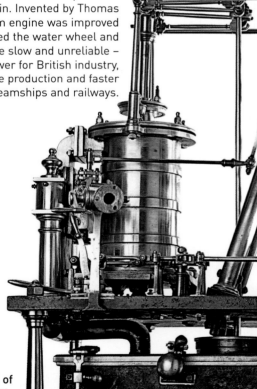

Model of James Watt's steam engine, which paved the way for the Industrial Revolution

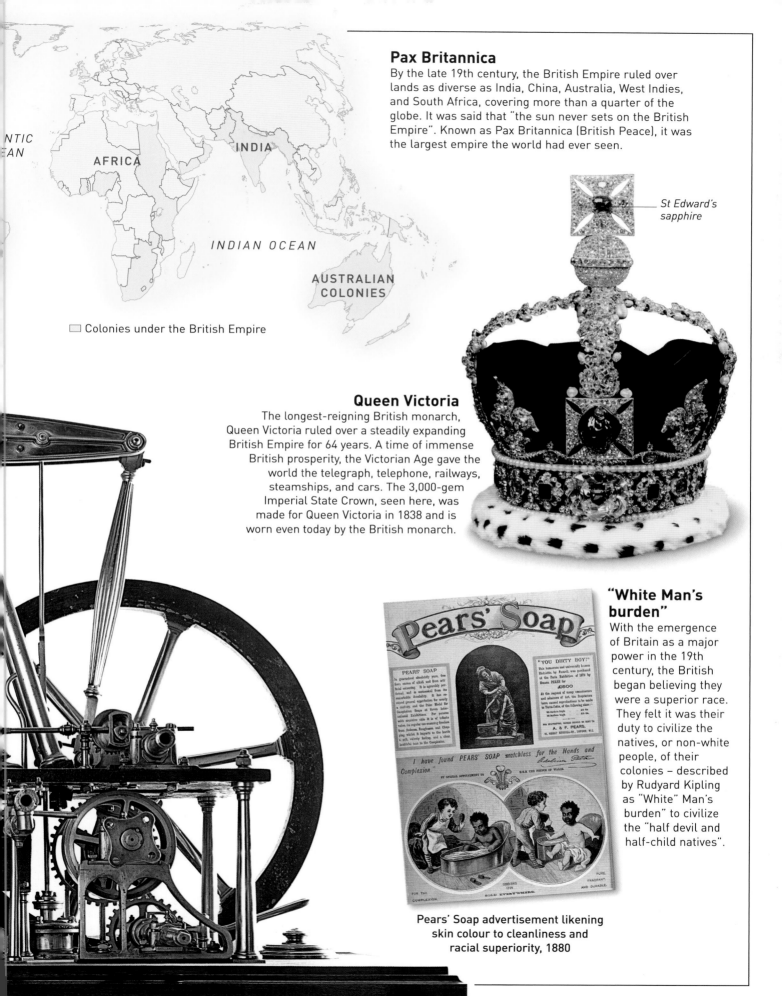

Pax Britannica

By the late 19th century, the British Empire ruled over lands as diverse as India, China, Australia, West Indies, and South Africa, covering more than a quarter of the globe. It was said that "the sun never sets on the British Empire". Known as Pax Britannica (British Peace), it was the largest empire the world had ever seen.

AFRICA

INDIA

INDIAN OCEAN

AUSTRALIAN COLONIES

☐ Colonies under the British Empire

St Edward's sapphire

Queen Victoria

The longest-reigning British monarch, Queen Victoria ruled over a steadily expanding British Empire for 64 years. A time of immense British prosperity, the Victorian Age gave the world the telegraph, telephone, railways, steamships, and cars. The 3,000-gem Imperial State Crown, seen here, was made for Queen Victoria in 1838 and is worn even today by the British monarch.

"White Man's burden"

With the emergence of Britain as a major power in the 19th century, the British began believing they were a superior race. They felt it was their duty to civilize the natives, or non-white people, of their colonies – described by Rudyard Kipling as "White" Man's burden" to civilize the "half devil and half-child natives".

Pears' Soap

Pears' Soap advertisement likening skin colour to cleanliness and racial superiority, 1880

Early years
(1869–87)

Mohandas, aged seven, posing for a studio photograph

Mohandas Karamchand Gandhi was born on 2 October 1869 in Porbandar, a seaside town in the province of Gujarat. He grew up in British India, in the princely states of Porbandar and Rajkot. A shy and physically weak boy, Mohandas hardly seemed to be the one who would challenge the British Empire 50 years later. However, this truth-loving child showed many signs of becoming a "Mahatma", or "great soul".

In the family
Karamchand, Mohandas's father, served as the prime minister of the Porbandar and Rajkot princely states. Liberal for his times, Karamchand had friends from all religions. Mohandas's mother, Putlibai, was a pious woman who regularly visited temples and observed rigorous fasts.

Childhood memories
Lovingly called "Monia", Mohandas was his parents' youngest child. Often up to some mischief, he and his friends once tried to steal a statue from a temple, but were caught by the priest. While his friends denied any part in the prank, six-year-old Mohandas owned up to it.

"The outstanding impression my mother has left on my memory is that of saintliness. She was deeply religious."

MAHATMA GANDHI
In his autobiography, *The Story of My Experiments with Truth*, 1927

Gandhi's father, Karamchand, and mother, Putlibai

School years
An average but diligent student, Mohandas studied at Alfred High School in Rajkot. During a school inspection, he misspelled the word "kettle" and was prompted by his teacher to copy the word from another student. But the honest boy refused to do so.

Early marriage
In keeping with the norms of his time, Mohandas, at the age of 13, was married to Kastur Kapadia, also of the same age. While the young husband wanted to educate his illiterate wife, an opinionated Kastur refused to be taught by him, preferring to play with her friends.

A much older Gandhi and his wife, Kastur, 1915

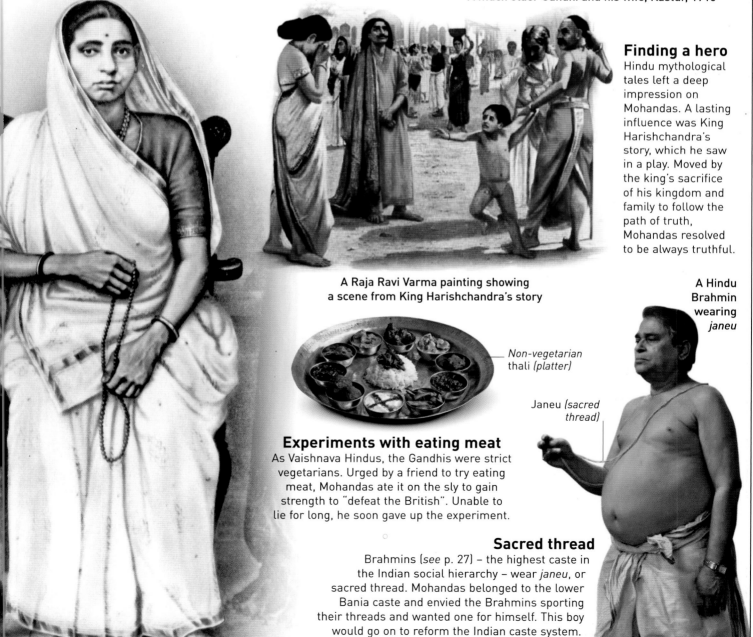

Finding a hero
Hindu mythological tales left a deep impression on Mohandas. A lasting influence was King Harishchandra's story, which he saw in a play. Moved by the king's sacrifice of his kingdom and family to follow the path of truth, Mohandas resolved to be always truthful.

A Raja Ravi Varma painting showing a scene from King Harishchandra's story

A Hindu Brahmin wearing *janeu*

Non-vegetarian thali *(platter)*

Janeu *(sacred thread)*

Experiments with eating meat
As Vaishnava Hindus, the Gandhis were strict vegetarians. Urged by a friend to try eating meat, Mohandas ate it on the sly to gain strength to "defeat the British". Unable to lie for long, he soon gave up the experiment.

Sacred thread
Brahmins (*see* p. 27) – the highest caste in the Indian social hierarchy – wear *janeu*, or sacred thread. Mohandas belonged to the lower Bania caste and envied the Brahmins sporting their threads and wanted one for himself. This boy would go on to reform the Indian caste system.

Mohandas in London
(1888–91)

At the age of 19, Mohandas Gandhi went to London to study law. However, he had to surmount some hurdles before his journey. Religious rules of the time forbade Hindus from travelling overseas. Also, his family fiercely opposed the idea of him living in a foreign land. His mother finally gave in when he took an oath of abstinence from meat, wine, and female companions. Mohandas sailed to England in 1888, the first person from his community to go overseas.

English gentleman
To fit into British society, Mohandas enrolled for lessons in dance, violin, and English elocution. He dressed as a fashionable Englishman, wearing a smart coat, a silk shirt, and a bow-tie. Later in life, he would call this phase an "infatuation" that lasted three months.

Living the London dream
Mohandas arrived in England in September 1888. Home to thinkers and philosophers, 19th-century London was stirring with ideas on socialism, women's rights, and universal religion, inspiring young Gandhi to form his own views on different issues.

The Big Ben and Westminster Palace, 19th-century London

Vegetables only

Mohandas's pledge of avoiding meat often left him hungry in his early days in London, as vegetarian food was hard to find. Fortunately, he soon discovered vegetarian restaurants and ate his fill. Later, influenced by Henry Salt's book on vegetarianism, Gandhi became an active member of the London Vegetarian Society.

Young Gandhi with other members of the Vegetarian Society at a conference in Portsmouth, England, 1891

Young Annie Besant

Sign outside the house in which Gandhi lived in London

Spiritual journey

While in London, Gandhi met theosophists Madame Blavatsky and Annie Besant, who believed in the pursuit of truth and universal brotherhood. He read Blavatsky's book, *Key to Theosophy*, which gave him a sense of the theosophists' respect for Hinduisim, and inspired him to read the *Bhagavad Gita*, an ancient Hindu scripture.

Simple life

Aware that his older brother had funded his stay in London, Mohandas adopted a simple lifestyle to reduce his expenses. He lived in cheaper accommodation, cooked his own food, and often walked long distances to save money on transportation.

Learning law

In Mohandas's time, clearing law exams by cramming notes was normal. However, Gandhi felt "it was a fraud... not to read these books". He even learned Latin to read original law texts. He earned his law degree from the Inner Temple, an association for barristers in London, on 10 June 1891.

Graduation certificate awarded to Gandhi

In South Africa

In 1893, Gandhi went to South Africa to assist an Indian firm in a legal case. At the time, South Africa was divided into British and Boer, or Dutch, colonies. Indians lived there as traders and labourers and were systematically discriminated against. Gandhi, a victim of racial bias himself, decided to stay on and help the Indians in South Africa in the fight for their rights.

Late 19th-century Southern Africa
South Africa was not a unified country when Gandhi arrived. It consisted of four provinces populated by native peoples, such as Zulus and Xhosas, but ruled by Europeans. Natal was a British colony, the Cape was a self-ruling British province, and the Transvaal and Orange Free State were independent Boer republics.

Model depicting the Pietermaritzburg incident

Not first class at all!
Gandhi was travelling in a first-class railway compartment from Natal to Durban to attend the court. At Pietermaritzburg, he was asked to get off the train by some white passengers who objected to "coloured" persons travelling with them. Gandhi refused but was thrown out of his compartment by a policeman. The incident inspired him to stay in South Africa and fight racism.

Indians or coolies?
Many Indians went to South Africa as "indentured labour", bound by an agreement to serve their employers in plantations abroad or at home. Most were Tamil- or Telugu-speaking people from southern India. Europeans contemptuously called them "coolies" or "samis", a corrupt form of *Swami*, a common Tamil surname.

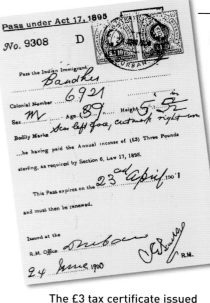

Pass under Act 17, 1895
No. 9308 D
Pass the Indian Immigrant
Bandhu
Colonial Number 6921
Sex M Age 89 Height 5 5 in
Bodily Marks Scar left face, cut mark right arm
...he having paid the Annual income of (£3) Three Pounds
sterling, as required by Section 6, Law 17, 1895.
This Pass expires on the 23rd April 1901
and must then be renewed.
Issued at the
R.M. Office Durban
24 June 1900 R.M.

The £3 tax certificate issued
to Indians in South Africa

Everyday racism

In the Orange Free State, Indians could only do underpaid jobs, such as that of a waiter. In the Transvaal, the authorities levied a heavy £3 tax on Indians. They could not own land or vote, and needed permits to go out. In 1894, Natal tried to introduce a £2.5 tax on indentured Indians, who could not afford it.

Natal Indian Congress

To carry out sustained campaigns for the rights of the Indians, Gandhi and his colleagues formed the Natal Indian Congress on 22 May 1894. Gandhi explained its aim in two pamphlets, *An Appeal to Every Briton in South Africa* and *The Indian Franchise: An Appeal*. Eventually, awareness about Indian issues started building up.

From lawyer to activist

In 1894, Natal, where Gandhi lived, proposed a law to deprive the Indians of the right to vote. Gandhi cancelled his plans to return to India and helped the Indians in Natal organize protests against this injustice. Through petitions and press propaganda, they made their voice heard and united the Indians in South Africa.

Gandhi's statue at the Government Square, renamed Gandhi Square, Johannesburg, South Africa

Green Pamphlet and its fallout

During his visit to India in 1896, Gandhi wrote the "Green Pamphlet" (so called beacuse of its green cover), bringing attention to the prejudice faced by Indians in South Africa. Widely publicized, it incited a white mob to try and lynch Gandhi when he returned to Durban. Pelted with stones and eggs, he escaped with the help of the local police.

Boer War medal

Satyagraha begins

Between 1903 and 1914, Gandhi launched and developed *satyagraha*, or truth-force, in South Africa to protest against the laws that were unjust to Indians. *Satyagraha* is a philosophy of peaceful protest in which the protester stays non-violent despite provocation. Thousands of Indians responded to Gandhi by disobeying laws and courting arrest peacefully, especially in the Transvaal, which had become a British colony after the Boer War in 1902.

Ambulance corps

During the Anglo-Boer War (1899–1902), fought between the British and Dutch settlers in South Africa, Gandhi raised an ambulance corps to provide medical aid for wounded British soldiers. He felt that this show of loyalty towards the Empire would ensure equal rights for the Indians in South Africa. Gandhi was awarded a medal for his services. He provided similar services during the Zulu Rebellion in 1906.

Indian Opinion is born

A journal called *Indian Opinion* was started in 1903 in Durban with Gandhi's support. Published in four languages – English, Hindi, Tamil, and Gujarati – it became the Indian voice in South Africa. In 1904, to overcome a financial crisis, Gandhi shifted the printing press from Durban to Phoenix, a rural settlement outside Durban.

First edition of *Indian Opinion*, 1903

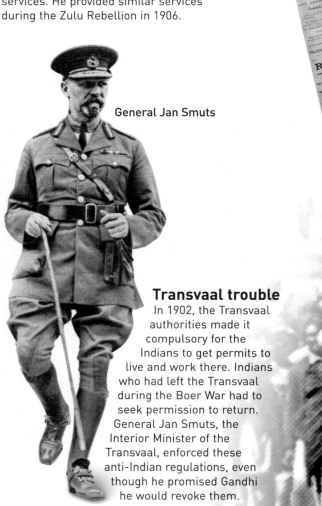

General Jan Smuts

Transvaal trouble

In 1902, the Transvaal authorities made it compulsory for the Indians to get permits to live and work there. Indians who had left the Transvaal during the Boer War had to seek permission to return. General Jan Smuts, the Interior Minister of the Transvaal, enforced these anti-Indian regulations, even though he promised Gandhi he would revoke them.

Burning protest

Led by Gandhi, the Indians decided not to submit to the harsh laws. On 16 August 1908, a massive protest was organized in Hamidia Mosque in Johannesburg, where more than 2,000 Indians burned their identity certificates in a cauldron. Several Indians, including Gandhi, were sent to the prison, an event that drew a lot of media attention.

Gandhi's original Transvaal Asiatic Registration Certificate

Replica of the cauldron, commemorating the 1908 protest, Hamidia Mosque, Johannesburg

Drama in two acts

In 1907, Gandhi led a mass protest against two unfair, anti-Indian acts passed by the Transvaal authorities. Besides denying entry to new Indians coming to the state, these acts made it compulsory for the Indians to register with the authorities, record their fingerprints, and always carry their identification certificates.

Great March

In 1913, the Transvaal authorities declared non-Christian marriages illegal. This was on top of an unfair £3 tax levied on the Indian contract labourers. In protest, Gandhi launched a *satyagraha*. More than 2,000 Indians went on a long march, courting arrest, and workers went on strike. On 7 March 1914, the Indian Relief Act abolished the tax and legalized marriages performed under Indian customs.

World influences

"I have humbly endeavoured to follow Tolstoy, Ruskin, Thoreau, Emerson, and other writers, besides the masters of Indian philosophy", said Gandhi in his book *Hind Swaraj*. He valued Western intellectuals. Indeed, many influences on his work came from philosophers and writers from all over the world. Gandhi merged their ideas with his own understanding of the world.

Suffragette Movement

When Gandhi visited England in 1906, the streets were packed with women demanding an equal right to vote, or suffrage. Admiring their courageous methods of protest, he urged the Indians of South Africa to learn from these women who were unafraid to go to prison.

Emmeline Pankhurst, leader of the Suffragette Movement, being arrested on 21 May 1914

Romain Rolland

Gandhi always corresponded with people from other countries, including the French writer and Nobel Prize winner Romain Rolland (1866–1944), who kept Gandhi in touch with developments in Europe. Deeply critical of imperialism, he was influenced by Gandhi's philosophy of non-violence. In 1924, Rolland wrote a short biography of Gandhi.

Henry David Thoreau

Another writer Gandhi admired was Henry David Thoreau (1817–62), who outlined the idea of civil disobedience. Thoreau said that it was the duty of people to peacefully resist any unjust government, a principle that shaped Gandhi's idea of *satyagraha*.

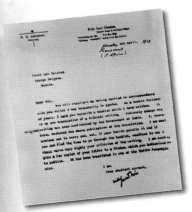

Thoreau advocated a life close to nature and lived in this house near Walden Pond, Massachusetts, USA

Leo Tolstoy

The writer of literary classics such as *War and Peace* and *Anna Karenina*, the Russian novelist Leo Tolstoy (1878–1910) inspired Gandhi with his religious-philosophical work *The Kingdom of God is Within You*, in which Tolstoy asked people to follow the teachings of Jesus Christ. The two men corresponded with each other through letters.

John Ruskin

The British thinker who affected Gandhi most profoundly was John Ruskin (1819–1900). Stirred by his book *Unto This Last*, Gandhi decided to put its principles into practice right away. He started the Phoenix farm in South Africa, where all people were considered equal and the same value was attached to all work, whether intellectual or menial.

St Matthew's portrait in Old Trinity Church, Massachusetts, USA

Lord Krishna

Arjuna

Spiritual influences

Gandhi often cited the *Bhagavad Gita*, a Hindu religious poem, part of the epic *Mahabharata*, and the "Sermon on the Mount" in the Bible among his spiritual influences. While the former carries Lord Krishna's teachings about selfless action, the latter contains Jesus Christ's lessons on love and compassion.

A scene from the *Mahabharata* showing Lord Krishna sermonizing Arjuna, the warrior prince, about selfless action, which formed the basis for the *Bhagavad Gita*

Portrait of the Raj

In 1600, the British Crown gave the English East India Company (EIC) the sole right to trade with India. The profits were so huge that the Company fought battles with the French, Dutch, and Portuguese to gain control over the subcontinent. By 1857, the Mughal Empire had weakened, and the British Crown began direct rule over India, a phase in history known as the British Raj.

English EIC coat of arms

English East India Company

The Mughal Emperor Jehangir gave the Company concessions to trade in India, allowing it to gain a vital foothold in the country. Later, the English EIC sought and received permission to collect taxes, build forts, raise an army, and mint its own currency. By 1833, the Company was ruling most of India in the name of the British Crown.

Economics and the Raj

The British made the Indian farmers grow cash crops, such as cotton, which they bought at cheap rates and sold at a profit. They did not allow local industries to develop, forcing Indians to buy finished goods imported from Britain.

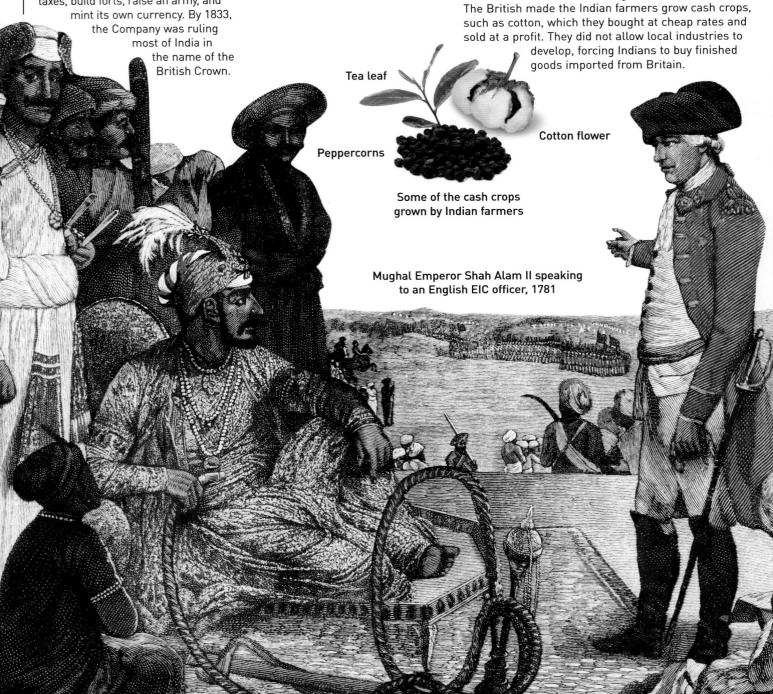

Tea leaf

Peppercorns

Cotton flower

Some of the cash crops grown by Indian farmers

Mughal Emperor Shah Alam II speaking to an English EIC officer, 1781

Rebel soldiers (on foot) fighting those loyal to the Company, 1857

Revolt of 1857

The Indian soldiers of the Company were unhappy about the racial discrimination they faced in the army and the unjust takeovers of some princely states, such as Awadh and Jhansi. They finally revolted when they were asked to bite open cartridges greased with beef and pork fat, which was against their religious beliefs. The revolt was crushed brutally by the British forces.

Doubting Thomas

Thomas Babington Macaulay, a British official, argued to replace Persian and Sanskrit with English as the medium of instruction in Indian schools. He wanted Indians to learn modern ideas and adopt Western ways. Ignorant of the Indian civilization, he maintained that European knowledge was superior.

Princely states

Even as the British ruled India, there existed nearly 565 kingdoms, or princely states, such as Mysore and Baroda, in India. The rulers of these kingdoms helped the British collect revenue and offered them military help. In return, they enjoyed nominal powers, received titles, and amassed huge personal wealth.

Stamp featuring Maharaja Sir Ganga Singh, ruler of Bikaner, a princely state

Manufactured in 1855, the *Fairy Queen* survives as the world's oldest working railway engine

Advent of modern technology

Technological innovations in the late 19th century united Indians like never before. While railways connected the country, the press brought information from all over India. Aware and educated Indians came together to form the Indian National Congress, the party that later spearheaded the freedom struggle.

Hind Swaraj

Gandhi wrote the book *Hind Swaraj* (Indian Home Rule) in 1909. Penned in Gujarati, and later translated into English, it was written in 10 days, while he sailed on a ship from England to South Africa. Composed in a dialogue form between the "Editor" and the "Reader", the book spoke about how to challenge British rule in India. It tried to spread the idea of non-violence among Indians.

Statue of Leo Tolstoy, Doukhobor Museum, Canada

Tolstoy's letter
The Russian writer Leo Tolstoy wrote "A Letter to a Hindoo" in 1908, urging Indians to refuse cooperation with the British, but without indulging in violence. Tolstoy's ideas inspired Gandhi to write *Hind Swaraj*.

Is civilization civilized?
In *Hind Swaraj*, Gandhi criticized the "Western civilization" marked by greed and temptation. He said that colonial empires were formed by gun power and motivated by the greed for luxury. India, he felt, should opt for simplicity; good conduct, not power; and non-violence, not force.

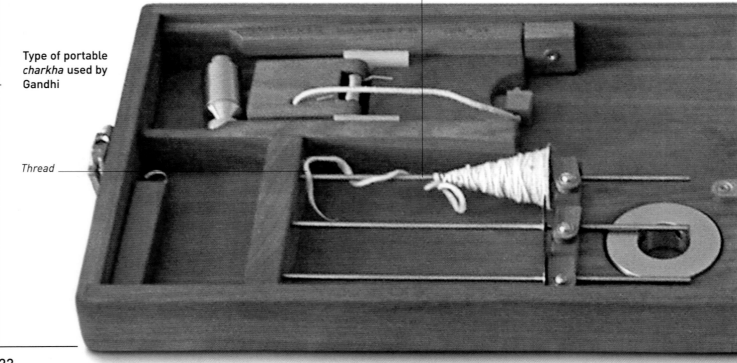

Type of portable *charkha* used by Gandhi

Spindle

Thread

Violence as protest

From 1905 to 1915, a wave of anger spread against British rule in India, resulting in violence. In 1909, Madan Lal Dhingra, a student, killed an English official, Sir Curzon Wyllie, in London. Gandhi urged young Indians to not support violence.

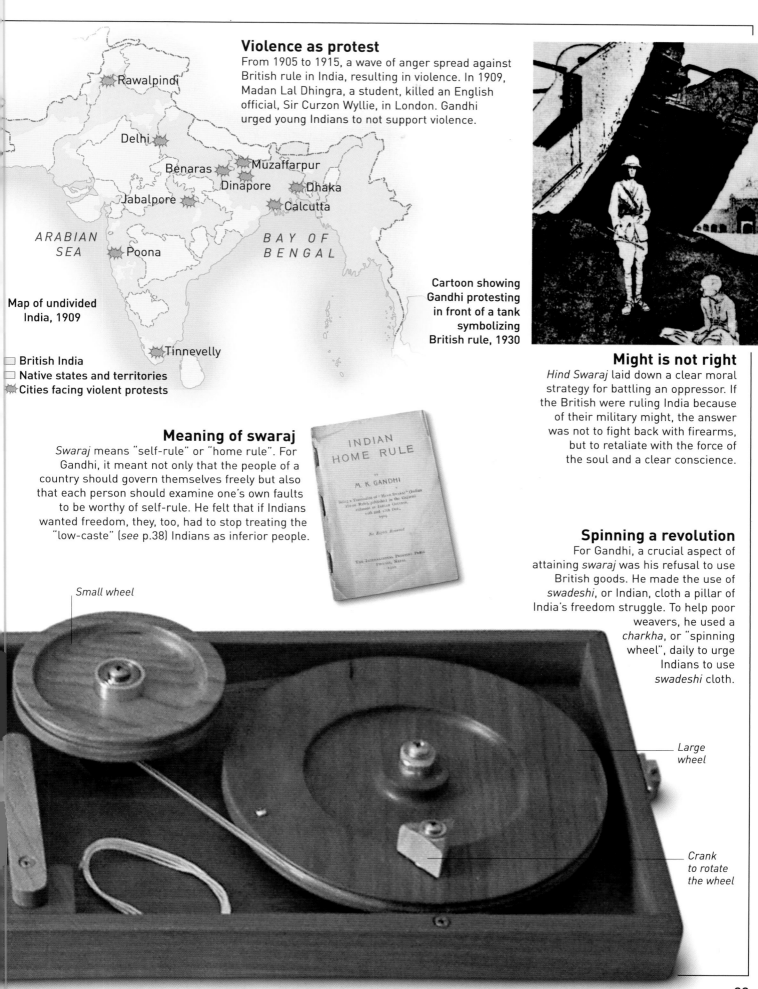

Rawalpindi

Delhi

Benaras
Dinapore
Jabalpore

Muzaffarpur
Dhaka
Calcutta

ARABIAN
SEA

Poona

BAY OF
BENGAL

Map of undivided India, 1909

Tinnevelly

☐ British India
☐ Native states and territories
✹ Cities facing violent protests

Cartoon showing Gandhi protesting in front of a tank symbolizing British rule, 1930

Might is not right

Hind Swaraj laid down a clear moral strategy for battling an oppressor. If the British were ruling India because of their military might, the answer was not to fight back with firearms, but to retaliate with the force of the soul and a clear conscience.

Meaning of swaraj

Swaraj means "self-rule" or "home rule". For Gandhi, it meant not only that the people of a country should govern themselves freely but also that each person should examine one's own faults to be worthy of self-rule. He felt that if Indians wanted freedom, they, too, had to stop treating the "low-caste" (see p.38) Indians as inferior people.

INDIAN HOME RULE

M. K. GANDHI

Spinning a revolution

For Gandhi, a crucial aspect of attaining *swaraj* was his refusal to use British goods. He made the use of *swadeshi*, or Indian, cloth a pillar of India's freedom struggle. To help poor weavers, he used a *charkha*, or "spinning wheel", daily to urge Indians to use *swadeshi* cloth.

Small wheel

Large wheel

Crank to rotate the wheel

Return to India

Gandhi returned to India from South Africa in 1915. India had become more politically active since he left it in 1893. To involve the common people in the freedom struggle, Gandhi travelled extensively across India. His interventions in peasant matters won him respect, and people began calling him *Bapu*, or "father".

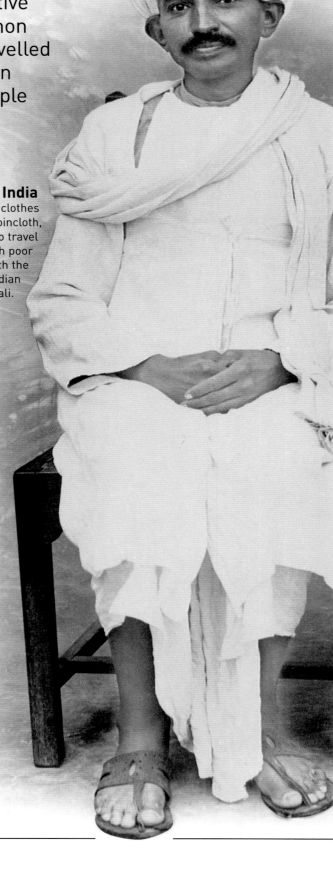

Indian in India

In India, Gandhi gave up European clothes and started wearing a *dhoti*, or loincloth, like common Indians. He chose to travel in third-class railway coaches with poor Indians. To connect better with the masses, he learned other Indian languages, such as Bengali.

Gopal Krishna Gokhale

An eminent Congress leader, Gopal Krishna Gokhale (1866–1915) was Gandhi's political mentor. Impressed by Gokhale's ideals of public service, Gandhi followed his advice to travel in India to understand the plight of common people.

Yarn dyed with indigo to colour it blue

Raw indigo dye

Bapu in Bihar

In 1917, Gandhi visited Champaran in Bihar, in eastern India, where British landlords were forcing peasants to grow indigo, instead of food crops, and to pay taxes in the time of famine. Gandhi mobilized the locals and courted arrest to draw attention to the cause. Eventually, the government stopped the forced cultivation and withdrew the unfair taxes.

Ahmedabad mill strike

In 1918, workers in Ahmedabad, Gujarat, in western India, launched a protest against mill-owners, asking for an increase in their salaries. Supporting the cause of the mill-workers, Gandhi went on his first political fast in India, pledging not to eat until the owners gave in. Soon, the workers got their desired wages.

Kheda satyagraha

Gandhi supported a peasant struggle in Gujarat's famine-hit Kheda district, where the government wanted to increase their taxes. In 1918, the peasants refused to pay, which led to many arrests. However, they stood their ground, forcing the government to stop levying the tax.

Mahatma Gandhi with social workers in Kheda, Gujarat

"The Kheda satyagraha marks the beginning of an awakening among the peasants of Gujarat, the beginning of their true political education."

MAHATMA GANDHI
The Story of My Experiments with Truth, 1927

— *Star of India*

World War I and India

Gandhi supported the British during World War I (1914–18), fought between the Allies (UK, France, and Russia) and the Central Powers (Germany, Austria-Hungary, and the Turkish Empire). Gandhi believed in the fairness of the British, and felt he could negotiate for better treatment of Indians in return for this show of loyalty.

Postcard showing various British colonies that participated in WWI

Names of Indian soldiers killed in WWI engraved on the podium

WWI memorial dedicated to Indian soldiers, Neuve Chapelle, France

Gandhi's ashrams

In 1904, on his way to Durban on a train from Johannesburg, Gandhi read John Ruskin's *Unto This Last*. Keen to put the book's message into practice, he founded a farm community in Phoenix, near Durban. Here, like-minded people led a simple life based on equality and dignity of labour. Determined to carry on his experiments with community-living after his return from South Africa, Gandhi set up ashrams, similar to Phoenix farm, in many Indian cities.

Replicas of the type of *khadau* (wooden sandals) worn by Gandhi

Sabarmati Ashram
Founded on the banks of the Sabarmati river in Ahmedabad, Gujarat, in 1917, Sabarmati Ashram was the centre of Gandhi's social and political work in India. Defining moments of the Indian freedom movement were conceived here. It was here that Gandhi began spinning the *charkha*, setting an example for Indians to make their own cloth.

Tolstoy Farm
Faced with the huge task of helping the families of *satyagrahis*, or protesters, jailed for defying the anti-Indian law TARA (Transvaal Asiatic Registration Act), Gandhi set up the Tolstoy Farm near Johannesburg in 1910. Named after the Russian writer Leo Tolstoy, the farm welcomed people of all religious and social backgrounds.

Charkha, *or the "spinning wheel"*

Gandhi's walking stick

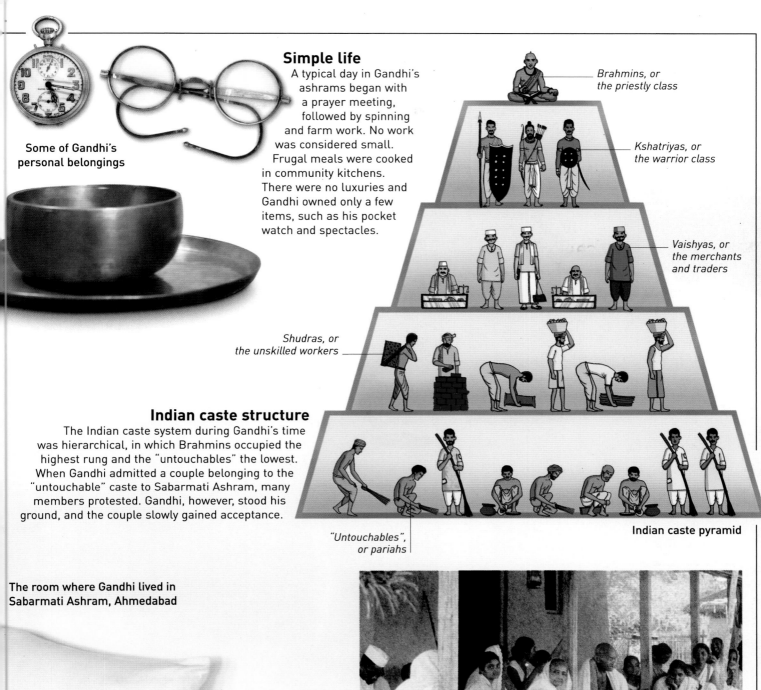

Some of Gandhi's personal belongings

Simple life

A typical day in Gandhi's ashrams began with a prayer meeting, followed by spinning and farm work. No work was considered small. Frugal meals were cooked in community kitchens. There were no luxuries and Gandhi owned only a few items, such as his pocket watch and spectacles.

Brahmins, or the priestly class

Kshatriyas, or the warrior class

Vaishyas, or the merchants and traders

Shudras, or the unskilled workers

Indian caste structure

The Indian caste system during Gandhi's time was hierarchical, in which Brahmins occupied the highest rung and the "untouchables" the lowest. When Gandhi admitted a couple belonging to the "untouchable" caste to Sabarmati Ashram, many members protested. Gandhi, however, stood his ground, and the couple slowly gained acceptance.

"Untouchables", or pariahs

Indian caste pyramid

The room where Gandhi lived in Sabarmati Ashram, Ahmedabad

Gandhi's writing table

Sevagram

Consisting of several small huts, Sevagram (Village of Service) in Maharashtra was the final ashram set up by Gandhi at the age of 67. Built in 1937 to serve the poor and "untouchables", Sevagram also became an important centre of India's political life.

Family and friends

"Whatever I am is because of her", said Gandhi of his wife, Kasturba. Apart from his wife and their four sons, he had a close circle of friends and disciples who were immensely loyal to him. They not only followed Gandhi but also helped him in his experiments with life and India's struggle for freedom.

Kasturba Gandhi

Ramdas Gandhi

Harilal Gandhi

Kasturba with her four children in South Africa, 1902

Trusted aide
For 25 years, Mahadev Desai (1892–1942), a lawyer and writer, served Gandhi as his secretary. He was always by Gandhi's side as his friend and confidante. He also translated Gandhi's autobiography, *The Story of My Experiments with Truth*, into English.

"Truly my better half"
When Kastur Kapadia (1869–1944) married Gandhi, little did she know that she would come to be respected as *ba*, or "mother", in her country. She led an active life, travelling widely, addressing public meetings, running ashrams, and being at the forefront of many a protest.

Bapu's children
Gandhi had a complicated relationship with his sons – Harilal, Manilal, Ramdas, and Devdas. Deprived of Gandhi's attention and care, they bore the brunt of his offbeat ideas. They did not attend school or have a comfortable upbringing. The eldest son, Harilal, renounced his family. The other sons, however, joined Gandhi in India's freedom struggle.

Soulmate

In 1906, Gandhi met Hermann Kallenbach (1871–1945), a Jewish architect, in South Africa. Both believed in dignity of labour and soon became close friends. Kallenbach donated 1,100 acres of land near Johannesburg for Gandhi's Tolstoy Farm. He visited Gandhi twice in India.

"Walking sticks"

Photographs of an older Gandhi often show him leaning on the shoulders of two young girls. They were his grandnieces, Manu and Abha, whom he called his "walking sticks". The two dedicated their lives to the service of Gandhi.

Devdas Gandhi

Manilal Gandhi

Friend of the oppressed

Charles Freer Andrews (1871–1940), a British Christian priest, came to India to teach philosophy. A great humanitarian and admirer of Gandhi's idea of non-violence, Andrews is respected in India as Deenabandhu, or "friend of the oppressed".

Finding a "treasure"

When Madeline Slade (1892–1982) joined Gandhi's Sabarmati Ashram in 1925, he said he had found "a treasure" and a daughter. Renamed Mirabehn, the Englishwoman became Gandhi's close ally, wore only *khadi*, and worked for India's freedom.

Mirabehn at a spinning wheel, 1940

A leader emerges

When the British introduced the Rowlatt Act in 1919, curbing the freedom of Indian people, Gandhi launched *satyagraha*, his non-violent method of protest, for the first time in India. In response to his call, Indians came out in huge numbers. The agitation was a great success, and it catapulted Gandhi onto the national stage. However, the unfair act and the Jallianwala Bagh massacre of innocent Indians made Gandhi lose his faith in the British. He now began to aim for self-rule in India.

"(Rowlatt Commission recommendations) are unjust, subversive of the principles of liberty and justice... If the proposed measures are passed into law, we ought to offer satyagraha."

MAHATMA GANDHI
On the Rowlatt Report, 1919

Rowlatt Act

Named after Sidney Rowlatt, the judge who drafted its provisions, the Rowlatt Act came into force to stop anti-British activities. People could now be arrested simply on suspicion and kept in prison without trial for up to two years. Freedom of the press was also curtailed as newspapers came under government control.

Gandhi and Kasturba arrive at a mass rally, 1931

Nation on strike

The protest against the Rowlatt Act took the form of a dramatic one-day nationwide *hartal*, or strike. Indians in every part of the country skipped work on that day to participate in the strike. Life ground to a halt, as shops shut down and schools did not function in response to Gandhi's call.

Jallianwala Bagh massacre

On 13 April 1919, a mass meeting took place in Jallianwala Bagh grounds in Amritsar, a town in northern India, against the Rowlatt Act. Brigadier-General REH Dyer ordered his soldiers to shoot at the unarmed crowd, which included women and children. Unable to escape from the enclosed park, more than 400 people were killed and 1,000 injured.

Tagore protests

Outraged by the Jallianwala Bagh tragedy, Rabindranath Tagore, poet and Nobel laureate, gave up the knighthood he had received from the British government. A commission was set up to look into the tragedy, but Brigadier-General Dyer was found not guilty.

Rabindranath Tagore Protest.

Against the Enormity of ment measures in the REQUEST TO BE RELI KNIGHTHOOD.

The following is the full text of the letter sent by S
His Excellency the Viceroy:—
Your Excellency,
"The enormity of the measures taken by the Gove
quelling some local disturbances has, with a rue
minds the helplessness of our position as British

News report carrying Tagore's letter to Lord Chelmsford, the then Viceroy of India

Gandhi takes centre stage

After the anti-Rowlatt *hartal*, Gandhi's stature grew. He was already a member of the Congress, the political party committed to fighting the foreign rule, but he now became its leader. In 1920, he wrote its new constitution, transforming it from a party of the elite to an organization of the common people.

Khilafat Movement

For all Muslims, the Sultan of Turkey was the *Khalifa*, or Caliph – their religious head. After Turkey's defeat in World War I in 1919, Muslims feared that the Caliph would lose his control over Islamic shrines. The Khilafat Movement was organized in India to voice Muslim outrage against the British government's anti-Turkey policy. For Gandhi, this was a chance to forge unity between Hindus and Muslims in India.

Ottoman Empire's coat of arms

Ottoman Empire
Ruled by a single family for seven centuries, the Ottoman (Turkish) Empire (1301–1922) stretched from Turkey to Egypt, eastern Europe, and West Asia. The Sultan of Turkey, the Caliph, controlled the Islamic shrines. When Turkey become a republic in 1924, the Caliph's position was abolished.

Procession of Khilafat supporters with a giant spinning wheel, Delhi, 1922

Hindu sacred chant "Om", in the Devanagari script

"Allah", the name of God, in the Arabic script

Gandhi addressing Hindu and Muslim volunteers, 1924

Hindu–Muslim unity

For centuries, Hindus and Muslims had coexisted in India, developing a common culture, even sharing a dialect, Hindustani – a mix of Arabic, Persian, and Sanskrit – still spoken in some parts of India. However, any friction between the two communities suited the British, who did not want them to unite. At Gandhi's behest, Hindus and Muslims formed a common front during the Khilafat Movement and displayed the strength of a united India.

Khilafat and Gandhi

"... I would be an unworthy son of India if I did not stand by them (Muslims) in their hour of trial", said Gandhi. In 1920, the Congress, the main Indian political party, and the Khilafat leaders agreed to fight together for the causes of Khilafat and *swaraj* (self-rule).

Movement begins

The Khilafat Movement gathered steam when the Ottoman Empire was partitioned under the Treaty of Sèvres in 1920, and most Islamic shrines came under British control. Muslim leaders urged people to boycott British goods and institutions. However, with the end of the Caliphate in 1924, the movement lost its main purpose and soon fizzled out.

Muhammad Ali Jinnah

A powerful Muslim leader, Muhammad Ali Jinnah opposed the Khilafat Movement, calling it an example of religious fanaticism. Jinnah until then was a member of the Congress and a votary of Hindu-Muslim unity. Later, he led the All-India Muslim League, a political party for Muslims and demanded a separate state for Muslims.

REMEMBER THY COUNTRY
IN THY PURCHASES
INSIST ON BUYING SWADESHI PAPER

Joker & Elephant
Brand equal in strength
and cheaper in prices
THAN FOREIGN
PAPERS

AND

SUPPORT INDIAN INDUSTRIES.

PIONEER
STOCKISTS
OF

ALL KINDS
OF
SWADESHI
PAPER.

TITAGHUR PAPER MILLS C L?

Non-cooperation
(1920–22)

Disappointed by the Rowlatt Act and Jallianwala incident, Gandhi launched the Non-cooperation Movement against the British rule. He travelled across India to explain his non-violent campaign. Thousands of people responded, turning the movement into a mass uprising. The British Raj was emphatically shaken for the first time and the goal of *swaraj*, or "self-rule", seemed within reach.

Non-violent boycott
The Indian National Congress and the Khilafat leaders adopted Gandhi's programme of "non-violent non-cooperation". People gave up their government jobs, students quit government-run schools and colleges, politicians avoided Raj councils, and volunteers courted arrest. Posters were printed, exhorting people to buy goods made in India.

A people stirred
Indians from all sections of society joined the campaign against the British. Students went to villages to preach *swadeshi*, urging people to use Indian goods. The Congress held public bonfires to burn foreign cloth. For the first time, women came out on the streets to protest, and nearly 30,000 people were arrested.

The Hindu symbol of swastika, believed to bring good luck

My country, my cloth

Gandhi spent some time every day spinning on his *charkha*. This was his message to his fellow countrymen to value manual labour and self-reliance. Gandhi saw spinning as a crucial means of earning a livelihood for the poor. Soon, *khadi*, or "handspun cloth", became the hallmark of India's freedom struggle.

Chauri Chaura Memorial, Gorakhpur, India

Chauri Chaura violence

On 5 February 1922, people participating in the Non-cooperation Movement at Chauri Chaura, a town in northern India, turned violent. Angered by police firing, they killed 22 policemen. Shaken by the violence and taking responsibility for it, Gandhi called off the movement on 11 February 1922. Later, on 10 March 1922, he was sentenced to imprisonment for six years.

"Non-cooperation with evil is as much a duty as is cooperation with good."

MAHATMA GANDHI
In a comment on the Non-cooperation Movement, March 1922

Women confronting the police in Bombay (now Mumbai), 1930

Reawakening

When Gandhi called off the Non-cooperation Movement in 1922, there was a deep sense of disappointment among his colleagues and other Indians. For the next six years, there was a lull in the freedom struggle. To fill the void and motivate people, Gandhi toured across India, recommending constructive work such as spinning, fighting untouchability, and strengthening community ties.

Gandhi's autobiography in two volumes

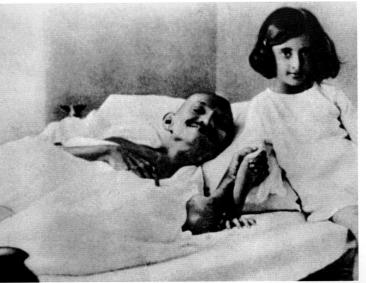

Gandhi with young Indira Gandhi, 1924

Prisoner, scholar, spinner
Convicted for inciting people against the British rule, Gandhi was imprisoned in 1922 at Yeravda jail in Poona (now Pune) in Maharashtra. Here, he read some 150 books, including Goethe's *Faust*. He also prayed and spun cloth regularly. After two years, he was released in 1924 to recover from surgery.

21-day fast
Gandhi came out of jail only to face an India where Hindu-Muslim unity of the Khilafat years was a fading memory. When Hindus and Muslims attacked one another in Kohat, a town in northwest India, Gandhi fasted for 21 days in Muslim leader Muhammad Ali's home, in September 1924. Among the many visitors who came to see the Mahatma was a young Indira Gandhi, the future Prime Minister of India.

Gandhi kept himself busy in prison by reading, writing, and spinning

My experiments with truth

In 1924–25, Gandhi published the memoirs of his non-violent movement in South Africa in serial form in his weekly papers, *Young India* and *Navjivan*. In 1925–26, he published his serialized autobiography called *The Story of My Experiments with Truth*. Everything that we know about Gandhi's life thus come to us through his own voice.

Protest denouncing the Simon Commission, Madras (now Chennai), in southern India, 1929

Charkha, *or the "spinning wheel"*

Simon, go back

In February 1927, a Commission headed by Sir John Simon was sent by the British to India to recommend how the country could be governed in the future. No Indian was included in the panel, forcing an angry Congress party to boycott it. People protested in large numbers, shouting the slogan "Simon, go back". They were brutally beaten by the police.

Father figure

Gandhi always tried to unite the different factions of the Congress. While senior leaders preferred a dominion status for India, remaining partly under British rule, younger leaders such as Jawaharlal Nehru pressed for complete independence. In 1929, Gandhi succeeded in getting Nehru accepted as the Congress president.

Gandhi and Nehru in Bombay (now Mumbai), 1942

Flag of freedom

On 31 December 1929, Jawaharlal Nehru unfurled the new Congress flag, with a *charkha* at its centre, in Lahore (now in Pakistan). This was a formal declaration that the party was committed to *poorna swaraj,* or complete independence. Gandhi fixed 26 January 1930 as the date when all Indians would pledge themselves to freedom.

Untouchability

A traditional way of organizing society, caste system is present in India even today, although it is losing its rigid hold. Under this system, society was divided into four hierarchical groups called *varnas*. The Brahmins, or the priestly class, formed the highest group; the Kshatriyas were the warriors; the Vaishyas were the traders; and the lowest class, the Shudras, provided manual labour. People who did the most menial tasks were considered "outcastes", or "untouchables".

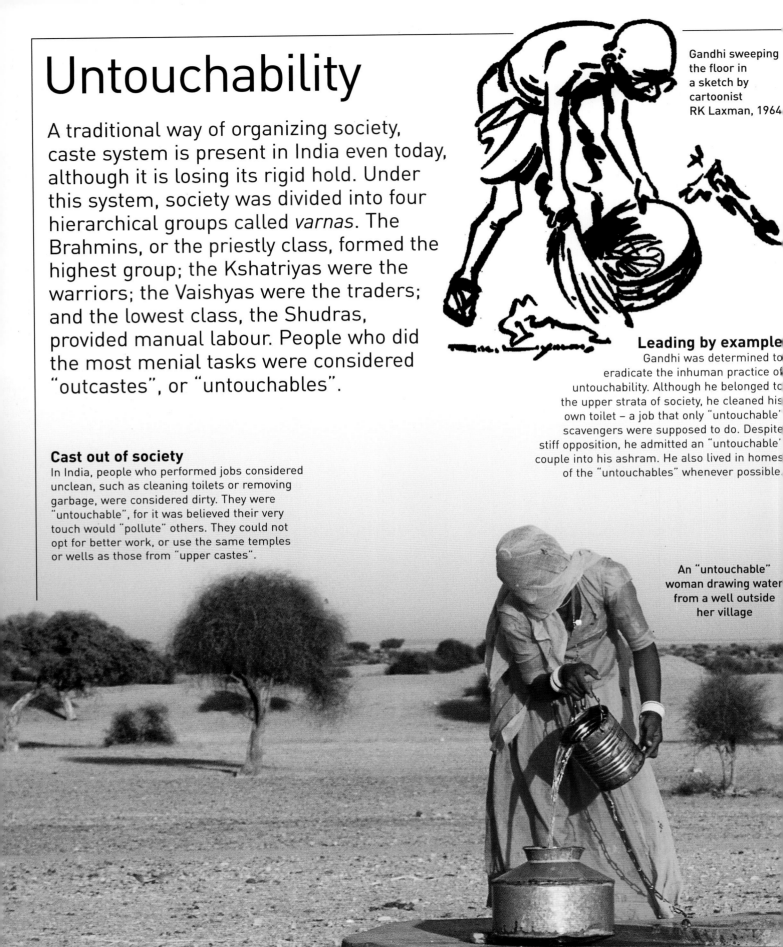

Gandhi sweeping the floor in a sketch by cartoonist RK Laxman, 1964

Leading by example
Gandhi was determined to eradicate the inhuman practice of untouchability. Although he belonged to the upper strata of society, he cleaned his own toilet – a job that only "untouchable" scavengers were supposed to do. Despite stiff opposition, he admitted an "untouchable" couple into his ashram. He also lived in homes of the "untouchables" whenever possible.

Cast out of society
In India, people who performed jobs considered unclean, such as cleaning toilets or removing garbage, were considered dirty. They were "untouchable", for it was believed their very touch would "pollute" others. They could not opt for better work, or use the same temples or wells as those from "upper castes".

An "untouchable" woman drawing water from a well outside her village

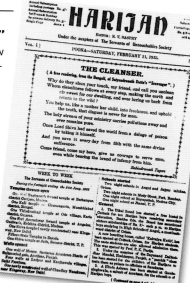

"Harijan"

In 1932, Gandhi gave a new name to the "untouchables" – "Harijan", or "Children of God". He started a newspaper called *Harijan* and formed the Harijan Sevak Sangh, an organization to work for the uplift of "untouchables". BR Ambedkar, however, thought the very name "Harijan" patronized the "untouchables" and made them "mere recipients of charity".

Vaikom satyagraha

A famous temple for Hindu god Mahadeva stands in Vaikom, Kerala, in southern India. The "untouchables" were not allowed to enter it or even walk on the roads around it. A *satyagraha*, supported by Gandhi, was launched in 1924 against this injustice. The "untouchables" tried to enter these roads peacefully, courted arrest, and faced police brutality. Eventually, three roads were opened to them.

Ambedkar's stance

In the 1920s, Bhimrao Ramji Ambedkar, from the "untouchable" community, emerged as their leader. He fought for untouchables' right to elect their own representative in the Parliament. In 1931, the British reserved some seats in the Parliament for the "untouchables", but Gandhi feared it would widen the caste divide and went on a fast in protest, forcing Ambedkar to withdraw his demand.

"Untouchables" today

The Constitution of India abolished untouchability in 1950. To improve the condition of the "untouchables", a portion of government jobs and educational seats have been reserved for the "untouchables", now called Scheduled Castes or Dalits. Despite these measures, they continue to face social segregation and violence, especially in rural areas.

Gandhi and his peers

Although Gandhi was the unquestioned political leader and moral authority in the Congress party and the freedom movement, his contemporaries did not hesitate to express their differences on questions of goals and strategy. When Gandhi withdrew the Non-cooperation Movement in 1922, or when he wanted to support the British during World War II, most Congress leaders disagreed with him. He found himself islolated when he proposed Jinnah's name for the prime ministership of free India.

Nightingale of India
Popularly called the "Nightingale of India", Sarojini Naidu (1879–1949) was a poet and a freedom fighter. In 1925, she became the first woman president of the Congress party. She played an active role in the Dandi March and Quit India Movement.

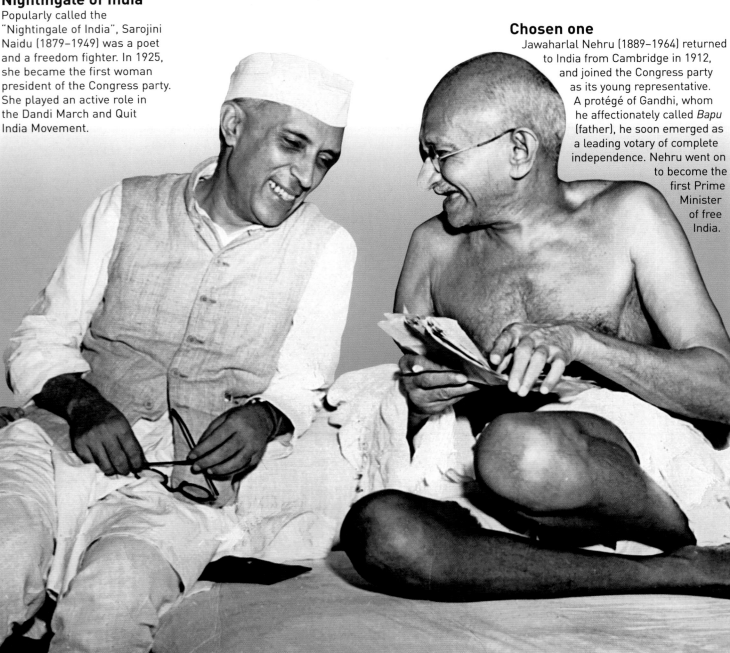

Chosen one
Jawaharlal Nehru (1889–1964) returned to India from Cambridge in 1912, and joined the Congress party as its young representative. A protégé of Gandhi, whom he affectionately called *Bapu* (father), he soon emerged as a leading votary of complete independence. Nehru went on to become the first Prime Minister of free India.

Conscience keeper

Affectionately called Rajaji, C Rajagopalachari (1878–1972) was a Congress leader and freedom fighter. A dedicated participant in the Non-cooperation and Dandi March struggles, he opposed Gandhi's Quit India movement, saying the Congress should negotiate with the British. Gandhi called him the "voice of my conscience". Rajaji was the first Governor-General of free India from 1948 to 1950.

Champion of Muslims

Trained as a barrister, Muhammad Ali Jinnah (1876–1948) began his political career with the Congress party. He left the party in 1920, unhappy with Gandhi's *satyagraha* methods. He became the Muslim League's permanent president and, by 1940, demanded a separate state for Indian Muslims.

Pakistani one-rupee coin depicting Muhammad Ali Jinnah

Dissenting voice

Congress president in 1938 and 1939, Subhas Chandra Bose (1897–1945) left the party in 1939. A committed patriot, Bose differed from Gandhi, believing that Indians should wage an armed struggle against the British. During World War II, he allied with the Japanese to fight for India's freedom.

Iron Man of India

Vallabhbhai Patel (1875–1950) gave up his law practice to join the freedom struggle. As a foremost Congress leader, he led peasant struggles against heavy taxes in Gujarat, forcing the British to revoke them. Patel became free India's first Home Minister. Often referred to as the "Iron Man of India", he worked hard to keep India united.

"Frontier Gandhi"

Khan Abdul Ghaffar Khan (1890–1988) was a political leader of the Pashtun people in the erstwhile North-West Frontier Province (now in Pakistan). A freedom fighter and a social reformer, he was so committed to non-violence that he was called the "Frontier Gandhi". His organization – the *Khudai Khidmatgar* (Servants of God) – worked for India's freedom.

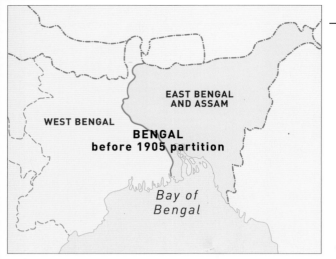

BENGAL
before 1905 partition

WEST BENGAL

EAST BENGAL
AND ASSAM

Bay of
Bengal

Roads to freedom

While the Mahatma's non-violent method of struggle fired the imagination of many Indians, there were people who followed other approaches to attaining India's freedom. Even before Gandhi arrived on the political scene, the Congress party had witnessed disagreements over which path to pursue. Old-timers preferred to politely petition the British, while others favoured agitations. From 1905, assassinations and bombings also found some takers.

Birth of militancy

In 1905, Viceroy Lord Curzon enforced a partition of the Bengal province, saying it was too big. This was seen as a hateful British attempt to "divide and rule" India since Bengal was a centre of Indian nationalism. Bengali anger gave birth to India's first militant freedom fighters, such as Aurobindo Ghose, and popularized protest methods, such as bonfires of British goods.

Moderates and extremists

The Indian National Congress was founded in 1885 to promote the participation of educated Indians in India's governance. In 1907, the party split into two factions – the "moderates", who petitioned the British, and the "extremists", who demanded self-rule. Extremist leader, Bal Gangadhar Tilak, was one of the first to say, "*Swaraj* is my birthright, and I shall have it!"

**Statue of
Bal Gangadhar Tilak**

Communist symbols hammer and sickle represent the working class

Communists

Formed in 1920, under the leadership of MN Roy, the Communist Party of India saw itself as the voice of poor Indian workers. It was often in opposition to the Congress, which it considered a party of elites. The communists supported the British in World War II, which made them unpopular with nationalist Indians.

Path of revolution

A young freedom fighter, Bhagat Singh (1907–31) was accused of murdering a British police officer. Along with Batukeshwar Dutt, he threw bombs in the Central Legislative Assembly in Delhi in 1929. He used his trial to spread the message of India's freedom, and went on a hunger strike to demand fair treatment for Indian prisoners. He was hanged in 1931 at the age of 23.

Poster supporting Bhagat Singh and Batukeshwar Dutt's hunger strike

Statue of Surya Sen

Chittagong uprising

On 18 April 1930, a group of revolutionaries, led by Surya Sen, a teacher, took over Chittagong (a town now in Bangladesh) for a day. They invaded British armouries, cut communication lines between Calcutta and Chittagong, and declared a temporary government. Sen and others were hanged in 1934.

Indian National Army

Impatient with Gandhi's non-violent methods, Congress leader Subhas Chandra Bose left India in 1939. During World War II, he joined the Axis Powers to fight the British. He even met Adolf Hitler for support. He formed the Indian National Army (INA) with Indians living in Malaya, Singapore, and Burma, and fought the British in northeast India.

Sleeve badge for a regiment of INA in Germany

Gandhi's letter appealing for support for the Dandi March

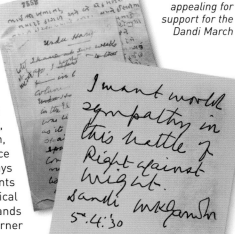

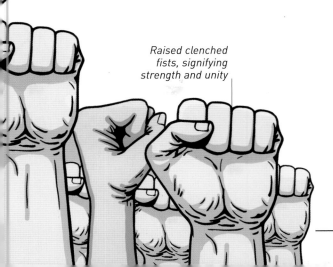

Raised clenched fists, signifying strength and unity

"Pen is mightier than sword"

As much as he admired the courage of revolutionaries, such as Bhagat Singh, Gandhi believed that violence caused only harm. He always negotiated with his opponents before launching a political struggle. He wrote thousands of letters and articles to garner support for the Indian cause.

March to the sea

On 26 January 1930, declaring complete independence as their goal, Indians pledged with Gandhi that "it was a crime against man and God to submit to British rule". Confident that people were ready for a new agitation, Gandhi launched another civil disobedience movement in March 1930. Aware that Indians resented the British government's monopoly to make salt, Gandhi based his new movement on this vital ingredient of the Indian diet. The agitation spread like wildfire, attracting volunteers from across the country.

All about salt

Gandhi had good reasons for disobeying the salt law, which not only prohibited the manufacture and sale of salt by Indians but also deprived the poor of their livelihood. Gandhi was also aware of the symbolic appeal of salt to people of all religions, castes, and classes. Making and selling it, in breach of the law, was a simple and effective method of protest available to all Indians.

Breaking the salt law

On 12 March 1930, Gandhi embarked on a historic march to Dandi, a village on Gujarat's seacoast. Gandhi and his associates left the Sabarmati Ashram to walk 354km (220 miles) to reach Dandi. Thousands of people joined them along the way. On 6 April, Gandhi lifted a fistful of salt and broke the law. Despite his arrest, the movement continued.

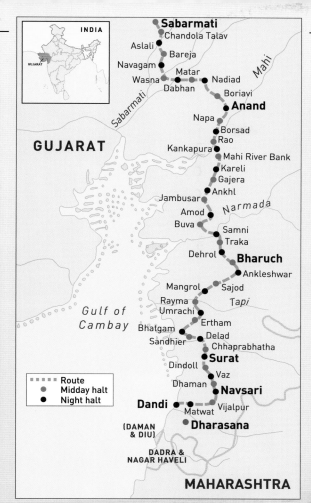

GUJARAT

INDIA
GUJARAT

Sabarmati
Chandola Talav
Aslali
Bareja
Navagam
Matar
Wasna
Nadiad
Dabhan
Boriavi
Anand
Napa
Borsad
Rao
Kankapura
Mahi River Bank
Kareli
Gajera
Ankhl
Jambusar
Amod
Buva
Samni
Traka
Dehrol
Bharuch
Ankleshwar
Mangrol
Sajod
Rayma
Umrachi
Bhatgam
Ertham
Delad
Sandhier
Chhaprabhatha
Dindoll
Surat
Vaz
Dhaman
Navsari
Dandi
Vijalpur
Matwat
Dharasana

Gulf of Cambay

Sabarmati

Mahi

Narmada

Tapi

(DAMAN & DIU)

DADRA & NAGAR HAVELI

MAHARASHTRA

Route
Midday halt
Night halt

Route map of the Dandi March in Gujarat (also showing Dharasana)

Police beating back protesters at the Wadala salt pans, near Bombay (now Mumbai)

Government responds

Indian protesters did not just openly make salt but also went on mass strikes and picketed foreign goods. The authorities responded to this civil disobedience with ruthlessness. They outlawed the Congress Working Committee, imprisoned more than 90,000 people – including Gandhi – and unleashed force on protesters.

Dharasana satyagraha

From Dandi, the movement spread to other parts of India. In May 1930, Gandhi declared a raid on the salt depots at Dharasana, 40km (25 miles) from Dandi. The volunteers marched peacefully but were brutally beaten by the police. Thousands were sent to jail.

Lord Irwin, Viceroy of India from 1926 to 1931

In the eyes of the world

The incredible courage of the marchers at Dharasana shook the conscience of the world. Reports appeared in many international newspapers and journals, such as *Münchner Illustrierte Presse*, a German magazine. Journalist Webb Miller's eyewitness report described how the police "rained blows... with "steel-shod *lathis*" while "not one marcher even raised an arm...".

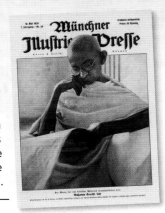

Gandhi-Irwin Pact

In February 1931, after his release from prison, Gandhi signed a pact with Viceroy Lord Irwin, which freed the salt march prisoners, allowed peaceful picketing of foreign goods, removed the ban on the Congress party, and permitted people in coastal areas to make their own salt.

Trip to England

As the only representative of the Indian National Congress at the Second Round Table Conference, Gandhi sailed for London in August 1931. Held by the British to discuss India's future with Indian leaders, the Conference proved to be a failure for Gandhi. His claim that the Congress represented all Indians was rejected by the other Indian delegates, and the British did not agree to his demand for self-rule. Nonetheless, he spent two months in England meeting people.

Gandhi disembarks from ocean liner *SS Rajputana* at Marseille's harbour, France, enroute to England

Round Table Conference

Indian delegates at the Second Round Table Conference in September 1931 included princes, religious leaders, and BR Ambedkar, who represented the "untouchables" – the lowest caste in India's social hierarchy. At the conference, many leaders demanded elections in which each community could vote for their representatives separately. But Gandhi was of the opinion that such a measure would further divide the people of India.

"... no matter what the fortunes may be of this Round Table Conference, I consider that it was well worth my paying this visit to England..."

MAHATMA GANDHI
Speech at Kingsley Hall,
East London, 17 October 1931

Cut from the same cloth

When Gandhi met the mill-workers of Lancashire, badly affected by the boycott of British cloth in India, the authorities feared that they would attack him. Instead, they talked openly to him. He listened to their problems and explained that they had "... three million unemployed, but we [Indians] have 200 million unemployed for half the year".

Gandhi being cheered by women from the cotton mills, Lancashire, England, 1931

Meeting Charlie Chaplin

In London, Gandhi met comedian Charlie Chaplin, the silent-movie star. Gandhi agreed to meet him when he was told that Chaplin honoured the poor in his films. Hundreds of people thronged to see the two famous men in Canning Town in east London.

Two sides of a 1931 British coin

Portrait of King George V

Europe calling

While in Europe, Gandhi spent time in Switzerland and Italy with his friend and biographer, Romain Rolland, who wrote of how "a hurricane" of people gathered to meet... the "King of India".

St Peter's Basilica, Rome, Italy

Mahatma and the Monarch

While in London, Gandhi was invited to an imperial reception by King George V and Queen Mary. Despite the protocol for formal attire, he attended the reception in his usual *dhoti*, or loincloth, which he wore to identify himself with poor Indians. When asked if he felt uncomfortable, he quipped, "The King has enough on for both of us".

World War II and India

World War II (1939–45) involved more than 30 nations and over 100 million combatants. Germany, along with Italy and Japan, formed the Axis Powers, who fought against Britain, the USA, Soviet Union, and France – the main Allied Powers. As a British colony, India sent more than 2 million soldiers to the war.

Swastika, emblem of the Nazi Party

Gandhi and Hitler

The main reason behind WWII was the ambition of Adolf Hitler, the dictator of Germany, who believed that Germans were a superior race and were meant to rule the world. Hitler's Nazi Party sent Germany's Jews to concentration camps where 6 million of them were killed. On 23 July 1939, Gandhi wrote to Hitler, asking him to "... prevent a war which may reduce humanity to the savage state".

Congress and the war

Many Congress party members wanted to offer support to the British in their war effort, but only in return for a promise of Indian independence. However, Britain involved India in the war without even consulting the Indian leaders. Gandhi eventually gave a call to the British to "Quit India". In return, the British propaganda machine accused Gandhi of supporting the Axis Powers.

World War II poster showing an Indian in the British army

Chiang Kai Shek with Franklin D Roosevelt

Indian National Army

Unhappy with Congress' support for the Allies, Subhas Chandra Bose left the party to form the Indian National Army (INA) to fight the British rule. Initially composed of the Indian prisoners of war captured by Japan during World War II, the INA fought against the British alongside Japan in northeast India.

Gandhi and world leaders

Gandhi wrote to both US President Franklin D Roosevelt and China's leader Chiang Kai Shek, saying that the Allied Powers could station troops in India to check Japanese aggression. He, however, pointed out that Allies' claim of fighting for freedom was hollow if Britain continued to rule India.

INA war medal

A British officer leading Indian soldiers in Egypt, 1940

Indian troops in WWII

Millions of Indian soldiers fought for the British in the war, in places as far-flung as northern Africa and the Middle East. They also fought the Japanese in Burma (now Myanmar) and near India's northeastern region, and played a key role in liberating Singapore and Hong Kong from the Japanese, who surrendered in 1945.

Quit India Movement

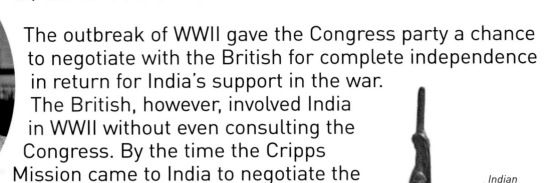

The outbreak of WWII gave the Congress party a chance to negotiate with the British for complete independence in return for India's support in the war. The British, however, involved India in WWII without even consulting the Congress. By the time the Cripps Mission came to India to negotiate the provisions for self-rule, Gandhi had already decided to launch another mass movement.

Indian national flag

Cripps Mission

By January 1942, WWII had reached India's doorstep, and the British were forced to seek Indian help. Sir Stafford Cripps, a member of the Winston Churchill's War Cabinet, came to India with an offer of a government that would include Indians in the Viceroy's Executive Council. Talks broke down when the Congress demanded that an Indian be the Defence Member of the Council.

"Quit India"

On 14 July 1942, Gandhi and other leaders met at Wardha, in western India, and passed a resolution demanding total freedom from the British rule. While members of the Congress supported Gandhi, the Muslim League opposed his move. The top leaders of the Congress party met again in Bombay (now Mumbai) on 8 August and voted unanimously in favour of the resolution.

Movement begins

On 8 August, Gandhi made a stirring speech at Bombay, exhorting people to "do or die" and urging them to "act as if you are free". Nationwide strikes and demonstrations followed. Some areas, such as Satara, in western India, established parallel governments, declaring themselves free.

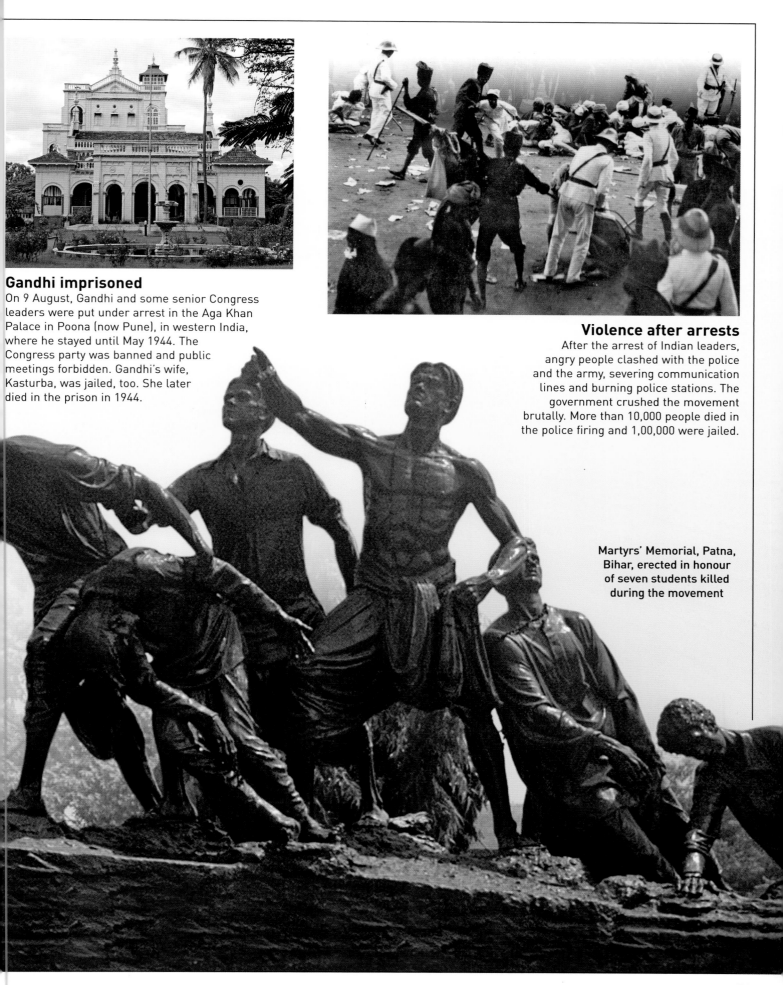

Gandhi imprisoned

On 9 August, Gandhi and some senior Congress leaders were put under arrest in the Aga Khan Palace in Poona (now Pune), in western India, where he stayed until May 1944. The Congress party was banned and public meetings forbidden. Gandhi's wife, Kasturba, was jailed, too. She later died in the prison in 1944.

Violence after arrests

After the arrest of Indian leaders, angry people clashed with the police and the army, severing communication lines and burning police stations. The government crushed the movement brutally. More than 10,000 people died in the police firing and 1,00,000 were jailed.

Martyrs' Memorial, Patna, Bihar, erected in honour of seven students killed during the movement

Search for harmony

Gandhi's vision of India was one of a country united. He spared no effort in bringing the Hindus and Muslims closer. Indeed, in the 1920s, the two religious communities joined forces to fight the colonial government with considerable success. On their part, the British did their best to aggravate the differences between the two religions.

Shared culture

Hindus and Muslims had lived peacefully in the subcontinent for centuries. The two religions were part of one civilization, sharing elements of food, clothing, architecture, and art. Indian architecture, for instance, often shows a blend of Hindu and Muslim styles. In Ganesh Pol, the arched gateway in Amber Fort, Rajasthan, floral patterns in the Islamic style flank an image of the Hindu god Ganesh.

Divide and rule

The British policy of "divide and rule" encouraged divisions between Indian communities. In 1909, John Morley, Secretary of State of India, introduced a system of "separate electorates", in which Muslims were able to elect their representatives in government councils separately from Hindus. This deepened the religious divide between Hindus and Muslims.

Members of the Muslim
League protesting in
London, 1946

Gandhi in Noakhali
Amid growing tensions
between Hindus and
Muslims, the district of
Noakhali in East Bengal
(now in Bangladesh) saw
widespread killings of
Hindus in 1946. Gandhi,
now aged 77, went to
Noakhali and walked
from village to
village, preaching
peace, repentance,
and forgiveness.
These efforts
restored peace
in the district.

Idea of Pakistan
Muhammad Ali Jinnah, president of
the All-India Muslim League, believed that
Hindus and Muslims were "two distinct
nations", indeed, "two different civilizations".
In 1940, the Muslim League asked for a separate
homeland – Pakistan – to be carved out of the
Muslim-majority areas in western and eastern India.

Frenzy of riots
Despite detailed discussions in 1946, the Congress party,
the Muslim League, and the British could not agree on
power-sharing between the two parties if the British left.
An angry Jinnah declared 16 August as "Direct Action
Day" to get Pakistan for the Muslims, which resulted in
a terrible bloodshed of both Muslims and Hindus in
several parts of eastern India.

Cabinet Mission

In March 1946, the British government sent three cabinet ministers to hold discussions with the Indian leaders about how power should be transferred to Indians. However, the Congress party leaders and Muhammad Ali Jinnah could not agree on how the Muslim-majority areas of India would be ruled. A partition of the country seemed inevitable.

Partition

From 1940 onwards, Muhammad Ali Jinnah and the Muslim League promoted the idea of a separate nation for Indian Muslims. For Gandhi, the idea was unacceptable. The other Congress leaders, however, became resigned to partition due to the rising discord between Hindus and Muslims. Independence thus came hand in hand with partition. Millions of people were uprooted, amid riots and killings.

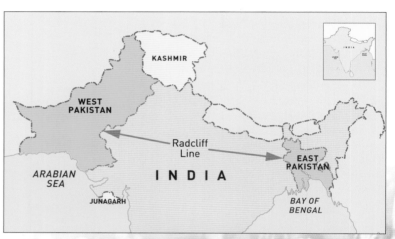

Map showing the areas carved out of undivided India to create East and West Pakistan

Radcliff Line

Sir Cyril Radcliff, a British lawyer, was invited to decide on the border between India and Pakistan. His task was to divide 4,53,200 square km (175,000 square miles) of land, rivers, roads, and about 88 million people. Radcliff, who had never been to India before, was given just five weeks to complete this work, and was in a hurry to leave because the climate did not suit him.

Mass exodus

Hindus and Sikhs from the newly created Pakistan migrated to India, and Indian Muslims to Pakistan, leaving behind their ancestral homes. More than 14 million people moved – on foot, bullock carts, and in inhumanly packed trains, with people spilling onto the roofs. Horrific killings took place on both sides of the border.

Indo-Pak wars
Gandhi had advised both young countries to work for mutual harmony and not embark on an arms race. However, the border region of Kashmir became a disputed territory from the moment of partition. India and Pakistan have fought four wars in 1947, 1965, 1971, and 1999.

Indian troops landing in Srinagar, Kashmir, 1947

One-man force
As India was partitioned, a saddened Gandhi chose to fast and hold common prayer meetings for Hindus and Muslims in Calcutta (now Kolkata), in eastern India. Lord Mountbatten, the last British Viceroy of India, said, "In Punjab we have 55,000 soldiers and large-scale rioting... in Bengal our forces consist of one man, and there is no riot".

Freedom at last!

After decades of struggle, India's independence was at hand. Exhausted by World War II, the British could not hold on to India any longer. In 1947, the British announced India's independence and also its partition into two countries – India and Pakistan. Violent Hindu-Muslim riots followed, saddening the Mahatma for whom the bloodshed took away any joy at achieving freedom.

Mountbatten Plan

Admiral Louis Mountbatten, the last British Viceroy of India, was in charge of overseeing India's independence. On 3 June 1947, he announced that if the legislative assemblies of Punjab and Bengal, where a majority of Muslims lived, voted for partition, the two provinces would be divided between India and Pakistan.

Pakistan is born

Under the partition agreement, Muslim-majority areas in the northwest and northeast of British India formed the state of Pakistan. The new country came into existence on 14 August 1947 – the date had a special significance for the Muslims that year. Muhammed Ali Jinnah was sworn in as the first Governor-General of Pakistan. He also came to be known as *Quaid-e-Azam*, or the "Great Leader", of the newly born country.

15 August 1947

On 15 August, India – albeit in its truncated form – became independent. In a stirring ceremony, the first Prime Minister of India, Jawaharlal Nehru, unfurled the Indian flag at the historic Red Fort in Delhi, setting a tradition for subsequent Independence Day celebrations.

Father of the Nation

On Independence Day, as India rejoiced, Mahatma Gandhi – the "Father of the Nation" – chose to remain in an abandoned Muslim house in Calcutta (now Kolkata), in eastern part of India. He mourned the partition and the terrible communal riots that followed by observing 15 August as a day of fasting and prayer.

"At the stroke of the midnight hour, when the world sleeps, India will awake to life and freedom."

PANDIT JAWAHARLAL NEHRU
On the eve of India's Independence, 14 August 1947

Border Security Force personnel at a flag-hoisting ceremony in Attari, Punjab

Independence Day celebrations

Every year, on 15 August, India celebrates its Independence Day. The Prime Minister hoists the national flag and gives a speech to the nation at the Red Fort in the Indian capital, New Delhi. Flag-raising ceremonies take place all over the country on this day. Indians also pay their respects to the freedom fighters who made it possible for them to live in a free country.

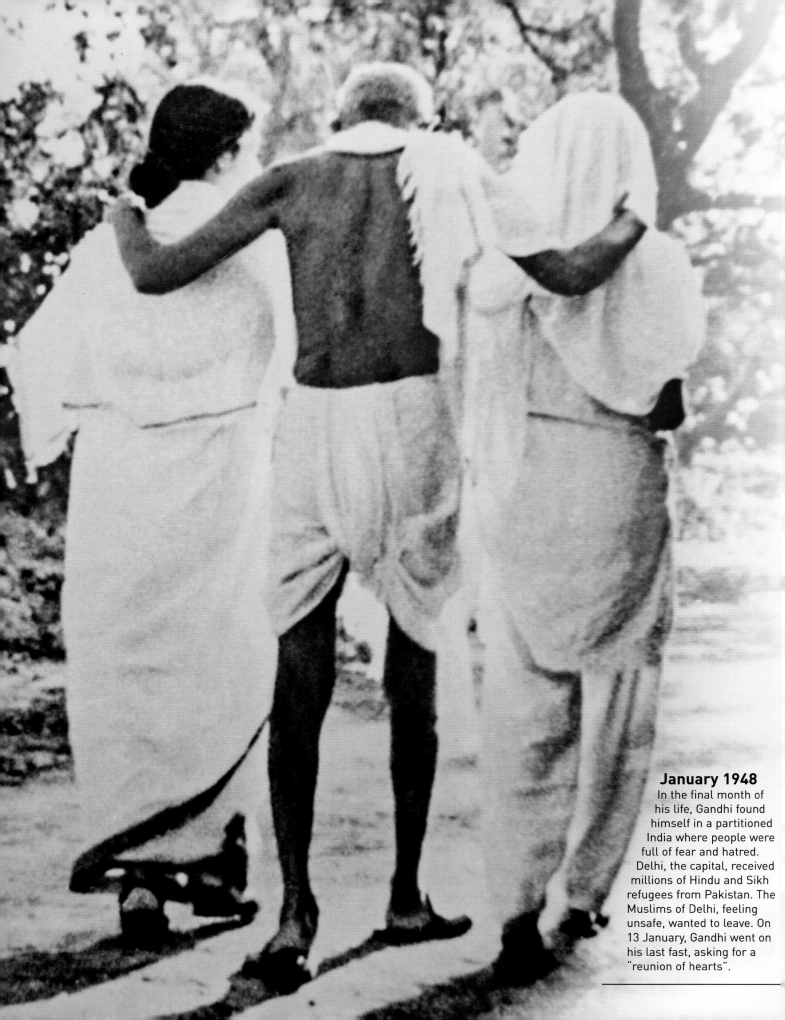

January 1948
In the final month of his life, Gandhi found himself in a partitioned India where people were full of fear and hatred. Delhi, the capital, received millions of Hindu and Sikh refugees from Pakistan. The Muslims of Delhi, feeling unsafe, wanted to leave. On 13 January, Gandhi went on his last fast, asking for a "reunion of hearts".

Gandhi killed

On 30 January 1948, Gandhi was at Delhi's Birla House, leaning on the shoulders of his grandnieces as he walked towards a prayer meeting. In the crowd stood Nathuram Godse, who fired three fatal shots at Gandhi. A Hindu nationalist, Godse blamed Gandhi for sacrificing Hindu interests and appeasing Muslims. Godse and co-conspirator, Narayan Apte, were hanged in 1949.

"Hey Ram!"

MAHATMA GANDHI
Uttering Lord Rama's name, moments before his death, 30 January 1948

Ashes to ashes

The news of Gandhi's death came from Prime Minister Nehru, who said on radio, "The light has gone out of our lives...". More than 2 million grief-stricken people joined Gandhi's funeral procession from Birla House to the Yamuna river in Delhi. Following Hindu tradition, Gandhi was cremated and his ashes immersed in the Ganga river at Allahabad, a city in northern India.

World reacts

"India Shaken, World Mourns" read the headline in the *New York Times*, as tributes and condolences poured in from world luminaries – the Pope, Albert Einstein, US President Harry S Truman, and England's King George, among countless others. They called Gandhi "a giant among men" whose death was a loss to humankind.

Gandhi's funeral procession,
6 February 1948

In Gandhi's footsteps

Even after his death, Gandhi has continued to set an example for people from all over the world, especially those struggling to change unfair and exploitative conditions in their countries. Leaders such as Martin Luther King, Jr; Nelson Mandela; and Aung San Suu Kyi found motivation in Gandhi's beliefs and strategies of non-violent transformation.

MANDELA RELEASED!

FREE ALL POLITICAL PRISONERS!

Martin Luther King, Jr
A pastor and leader of the Civil Rights Movement in the USA, Martin Luther King, Jr (1929–68) strove to bring social and legal equality to the African-Americans, who were denied equal opportunities and voting rights or access to public spaces. He acknowledged Gandhi's teachings to be his "guiding light".

Nelson Mandela
Inspired by Gandhi's methods of non-violent resistance, Nelson Mandela (1918–2013) fought apartheid – the policy of racial discrimination against blacks – followed in South Africa since 1948. He was thrown into prison for 27 years. He became South Africa's first black President in 1994.

Martin Luther King, Jr leading a march in Alabama, USA, 1965

Albert Einstein
Passionately opposed to war, Albert Einstein (1879–1955) was a great German physicist and Nobel laureate. He once wrote to Gandhi, "You have shown it is possible to succeed without violence...". On his 70th birthday, he said, "Generations to come... will scarce believe that such a man... walked upon this Earth".

"Christ furnished the spirit and the motivation while Gandhi furnished the method."

MARTIN LUTHER KING, JR
The Autobiography of Martin Luther King, Jr, 1998

John Lennon

Famous British musician, founder-member of the pop band The Beatles, and writer of stirring songs such as "Give Peace a Chance", John Lennon (1940–80) was an admirer of Gandhi and his principle of non-violence. Lennon and his Japanese wife, Yoko Ono, were peace activists who campaigned against the now-infamous Vietnam War.

WAR IS OVER!

IF YOU WANT IT

Happy Christmas from John & Yoko

Aung San Suu Kyi

Nobel Peace Prize winner Aung San Suu Kyi (b. 1945) has struggled for democracy and against military rule in her country, Myanmar, for much of her life. She has often cited Gandhi's life and work as her inspiration to fight the oppressive regime in her country.

DAW AUNG SAN SUU KYI

Congressional medal awarded to Suu Kyi by the USA, 2008

Barack Obama

"I might not be standing before you today, as President of the United States, had it not been for Gandhi..." The USA's first African-American President, Barack Obama (b. 1961), often quotes Gandhi as his inspiration to spread the message that we personally "be" the change that we seek in the world, and that ordinary people can do extraordinary things.

Non-violence in action

DAILY NEWS
NEW YORK'S HOMETOWN NEWSPAPER
1913-2005

ROSA PARKS

7053

She refused to give up her bus seat to a white man and changed America forever **PAGES 2-3**

For Gandhi, being fearless and not giving in to hatred were two crucial pillars of non-violence – a philosophy that continues to appeal to people across the world. The 20th century witnessed moments of intense political conflict in which ordinary people embarked on dramatic protests yet remained peaceful. From leaders such as Václav Havel to Lech Wałęsa, these activists showed how non-violence could transform the world.

Rosa Parks, USA

In the 1950s, African-Americans in the USA went to "blacks-only" schools. They had to vacate seats in buses for white people, if asked. On 1 December 1955, Rosa Parks (1913–2005), a seamstress and civil rights' activist in Montgomery, Alabama, refused to give up her seat on a bus and was arrested. Angry African-Americans carried out a year-long boycott of buses, forcing the government to abolish the law.

Solidarity Movement, Poland

Unhappy about the lack of freedom in communist Poland in the 1980s, people joined Solidarity – a trade union led by Lech Wałęsa (b. 1943). Enjoying the support of the Catholic Church, it organized mass strikes, without once turning violent. Wałęsa won the Nobel Peace Prize in 1983. When the government was forced to concede free elections in 1989, he became the President of Poland.

A 1990 coin issued to celebrate Solidarity's 10-year struggle

Flower power, USA

In an anti-Vietnam War rally in 1967, thousands of students marched to the Pentagon, the US Department of Defense, in Washington, D.C., and put flowers in the guns of soldiers as a mark of peace. The war, fought between North (supported by China) and South Vietnam (supported by the USA), saw innocent Vietnamese being killed, which evoked widespread anger in the USA.

Unknown protester blocks a military convoy at Tiananmen Square in Beijing, China, 1989

Tiananmen Square, China

In 1989, thousands of students gathered at Tiananmen Square in Beijing, China, to mourn the death of a liberal leader. When sit-ins and hunger strikes continued, highlighting the lack of freedom and corruption in China, the authorities imposed martial law and arrested hundreds of protesters. On 4 June, they sent military tanks, which killed more than 200 people, emphatically ending the protests.

Celebrating the date on which Velvet Revolution began — **17.11.1989**

Velvet Revolution, Czechoslovakia

Czechoslovakia (now the Czech Republic and Slovakia) had been ruled by the Communist Party since 1948. In November 1989, unhappy about the lack of freedom, students and workers went on an anti-government march. The police reacted with force, beating the protesters, who remained peaceful. This non-violent revolution resulted in the overthrow of the government. The same year, Václav Havel (1936–2011) was elected president of the new republic.

Lady in red, Turkey

In 2013, Turkey erupted into an agitation against the country's authoritarian government. Initially directed at the government's plan to destroy Gazi Park, a tiny green patch in Istanbul, the protests soon turned into huge demonstrations. As the police used force against protesters, Ceyda Sungur, a peaceful protester, was attacked with tear gas. Her picture became a symbol of the government's high-handedness, giving a boost to the movement.

Timeline

Gandhi's story is not an ordinary recounting of his life events. Whether it was his childhood years in Gujarat, the time he spent in South Africa, or the heady days of India's freedom struggle, these are phases in history that either shaped his world view or were influenced by his ideals.

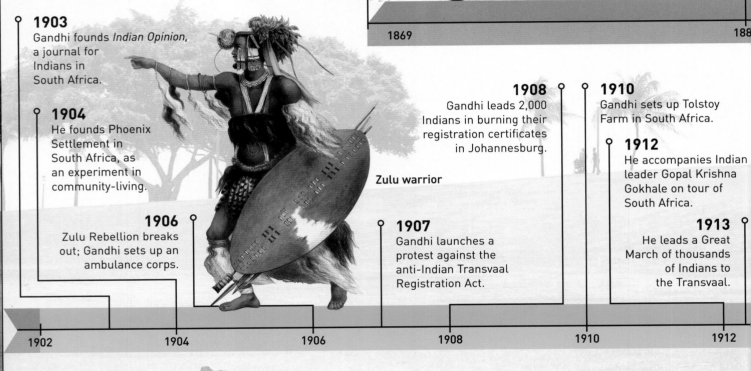

2 October 1869
Mohandas Karamchand Gandhi is born into a Modh Bania family in Gujarat.

Young Gandhi with his brother Laxmidas

1883
Mohandas marries Kastur Kapadia at the age of 13.

1869   188[?]

1903
Gandhi founds *Indian Opinion*, a journal for Indians in South Africa.

1904
He founds Phoenix Settlement in South Africa, as an experiment in community-living.

1906
Zulu Rebellion breaks out; Gandhi sets up an ambulance corps.

Zulu warrior

1907
Gandhi launches a protest against the anti-Indian Transvaal Registration Act.

1908
Gandhi leads 2,000 Indians in burning their registration certificates in Johannesburg.

1910
Gandhi sets up Tolstoy Farm in South Africa.

1912
He accompanies Indian leader Gopal Krishna Gokhale on tour of South Africa.

1913
He leads a Great March of thousands of Indians to the Transvaal.

1902   1904   1906   1908   1910   1912

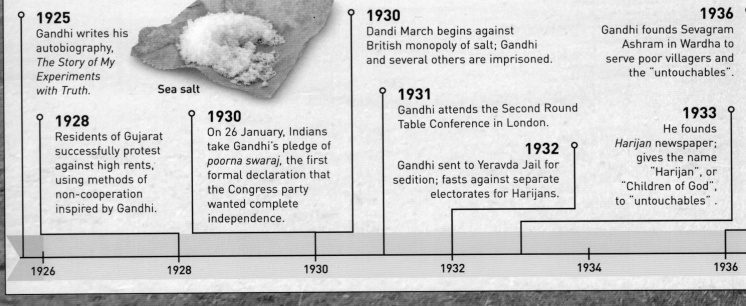

1925
Gandhi writes his autobiography, *The Story of My Experiments with Truth.*

Sea salt

1928
Residents of Gujarat successfully protest against high rents, using methods of non-cooperation inspired by Gandhi.

1930
On 26 January, Indians take Gandhi's pledge of *poorna swaraj*, the first formal declaration that the Congress party wanted complete independence.

1930
Dandi March begins against British monopoly of salt; Gandhi and several others are imprisoned.

1931
Gandhi attends the Second Round Table Conference in London.

1932
Gandhi sent to Yeravda Jail for sedition; fasts against separate electorates for Harijans.

1936
Gandhi founds Sevagram Ashram in Wardha to serve poor villagers and the "untouchables".

1933
He founds *Harijan* newspaper; gives the name "Harijan", or "Children of God", to "untouchables".

1926   1928   1930   1932   1934   1936

1888
Gandhi sails for London to study law despite opposition from elders.

1891
He joins the Vegetarian Society in London; passes the bar exam.

Gandhi in South Africa

1893
He leaves for Natal, South Africa, to help an Indian firm, Dada Abdulla & Company, in a legal case.

1894
He sets up the Natal Indian Congress, with other founder-members

1896
Gandhi returns to India from South Africa for the first time.

1901
He travels to India; makes efforts to garner support for the Indians in South Africa.

Tin can used to deliver food to the Boer War soldiers

1899
Gandhi organizes an ambulance corps during the Second Boer War.

1888   1890   1892   1894   1896   1898   1900

1914
Gandhi raises volunteer corps in London during World War I.

Poppy flower dedicated to the WWI dead

1915
He returns to India and travels across the country; founds Sabarmati Ashram.

1917
Gandhi supports the cause of Champaran's indigo farmers.

Jallianwala Bagh Memorial, Amritsar

1919
Amritsar massacre under Brigadier-General Dyer, British troops kill innocent protesters.

1920
Gandhi launches non-violent Non-cooperation Movement; India responds enthusiastically.

1919
Gandhi declares a national day of fasting against the Rowlatt Act.

1922
Gandhi arrested for sedition; calls off Non-cooperation Movement.

Handcuffs

1924
He is released from prison; becomes the Congress president.

1914   1916   1918   1920   1922   1924

UNITED

NATIONS FIGHT FOR FREEDOM

1942
Gandhi calls for the British to "Quit" India and is arrested.

World War II poster

1939
Congress party is divided over participation in World War II.

1943
Gandhi fasts for 21 days to protest against British rule, while in Aga Khan Palace prison in Pune.

1944
Kasturba dies in Pune; Gandhi is released from prison.

1946
Cabinet Mission arrives from Britain to work out the details of Indian independence.

"Hey Ram", Gandhi's last words, inscribed at Gandhi Smriti, New Delhi

1947
India gains independence; Country partitioned into India and Pakistan.

1948
Gandhi is shot dead by Hindu fanatic Nathuram Godse.

हे राम
५-१७- सायंकाल
३०-१-४८

1938   1940   1942   1944   1946   1948

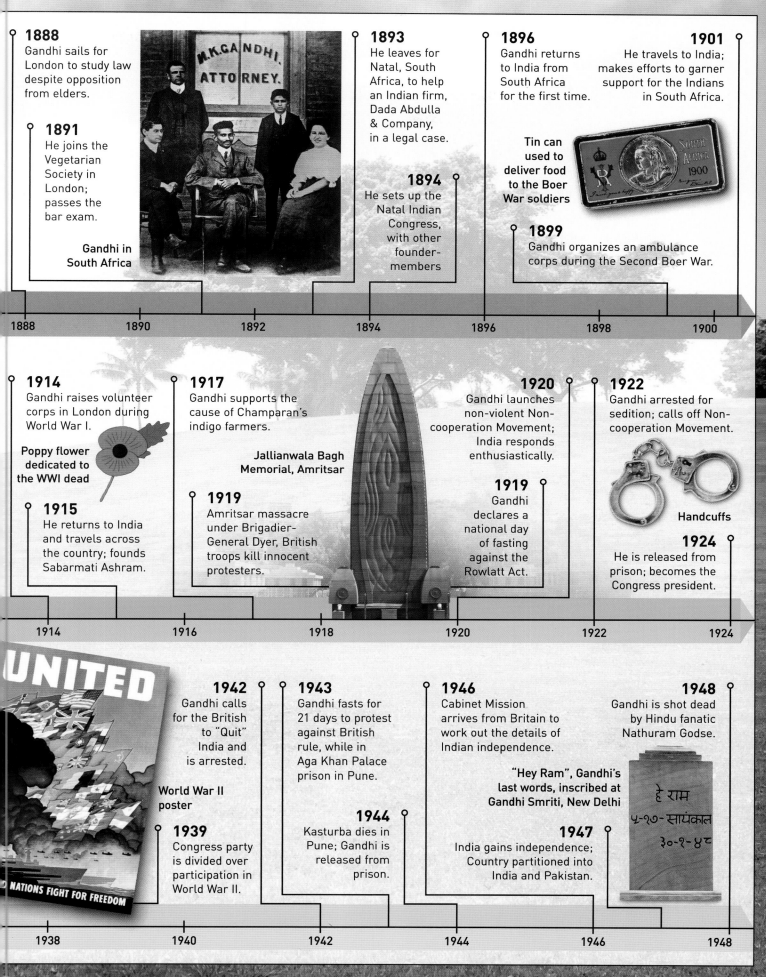

Did you know?

FASCINATING FACTS ABOUT GANDHI

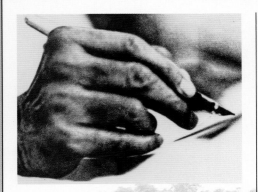

Gandhi was such a prolific writer that the compilation of his letters and articles, *The Collected Works of Mahatma Gandhi*, has been published in 100 volumes.

Gandhi was ambidextrous – he could write with both hands. He could spin with both hands as well.

When Gandhi first bacame a lawyer, he was so terrified of public speaking that he panicked in the courtroom and was unable to represent his client.

Gandhi shares his birthday (2 October) with American comedian Groucho Marx and with English writer Graham Greene. Marx and Gandhi wore the same kind of round spectacles, sported similar moustaches, and were known for their witty remarks.

Groucho Marx

India observes only three national holidays – Independence Day on 15 August, Republic Day on 26 January, and Gandhi's birthday on 2 October. His birthday is also observed as the International Day of Non-violence.

Five Nobel Peace Prize winners – Martin Luther King, Jr; Aung San Suu Kyi; Nelson Mandela; Adolfo Pérez Esquivel; and Barack Obama have acknowledged Gandhi's influence on their world view. Gandhi, however, never won a Nobel Prize.

World Peace gong at
Gandhi Smriti Museum, New Delhi

Exhibited in the Gandhi Smriti Museum, New Delhi, the World Peace gong commemorates the centenary of Gandhi's first *satyagraha* in South Africa in 1906. It depicts the flags of all member countries of the United Nations and symbols of world religions. It was presented by the Multi-Cultural Society of Indonesia in 2006.

Gandhi's footsteps, marking his final walk, at Gandhi Smriti, New Delhi

Gandhi was the first "coloured" lawyer to be admitted to the Supreme Court in South Africa. (Asians, who were neither "white" nor "black", were called "coloured" in his time in South Africa)

Gandhi joined the Second Boer War, in 1902, as Sergeant-Major. He fought on the British side.

Gandhi first came across a *charkha*, or "spinning wheel", in 1915, at the age of 46.

When Gandhi's wife, Kasturba, died in prison, she was dressed in a saree made of yarn spun by Gandhi.

Gandhi owned fewer than 10 items, including his watch, spectacles, and sandals. He stayed in ashrams most of his life and never owned a house.

Poster of the film
Lage Raho Munna Bhai

Several movies have been made on Gandhi. Richard Attenborough's *Gandhi* (1982) won eight Academy Awards – the highest for any movie inspired by a real-life personality. In India, Hindi movies *Lage Raho Munna Bhai* (2006) and *Gandhi, My Father* (2007) are two famous films based on Gandhi's life.

In 1930, Gandhi was *Time* magazine's "Man of the Year", and in 1999, he was the second-favourite "Person of the Century", after Albert Einstein.

Gandhi was sent to prison 11 times in South Africa and India. In all, he spent 6 years and 10 months in prison. In his later life, he looked forward to going to jail, where he could read and spin peacefully. Poet Rabindranath Tagore called it Gandhi's "arrest cure"!

Gandhi never visited the USA. Among his many admirers in the country was industrialist Henry Ford who sent him a letter praising his non-violent campaign against British rule.

Gandhi was a committed follower of naturopathy. When ill, he never took medicines, preferring to cure himself by fasting, massages, and special diets.

Garlic

Natural remedies advocated by Gandhi

Onion

Gandhi found great peace in nursing the sick. As a boy, he nursed his ailing father. He devoted two hours every day in a charitable hospital in South Africa, gave therapeutic cures to residents of his ashrams in India, and even dressed the wounds of lepers.

Once Gandhi was operated upon in prison. A British nurse teased him, saying, "You... owed your life to the skill of a British surgeon... administering British drugs and to the ministrations of a British nurse!"

Gandhi was an extraordinary walker. As a law student in London, he often walked for miles a day to save money. During the Dandi March, he walked 15km (9 miles) every day. At the age of 77, he walked barefoot from village to village for two months on his peace mission in Noakhali, East Bengal (now a part of Bangladesh).

Throughout his life, Gandhi changed his style of dressing to suit his beliefs. While studying in London, he experimented with a Western suit. In South Africa, he dressed in suits to impress the Europeans. On returning to India, he wore a *dhoti*, or loincloth, to be able to relate with ordinary Indians.

The co-founder of Apple, Steve Jobs, said that, for him, Gandhi was the "Person of the Century". Jobs always kept a picture of Gandhi with him. Apple's "Think Different" advertisement campaign featured an image of Gandhi.

Gandhi was extremely punctual. Before his assassination on 30 January 1948, Gandhi was upset that he was late for the evening prayer by 10 minutes.

Castor oil plant

Crushed turmeric

Turmeric root

Gandhi's funeral procession in Delhi was 8-km (5-miles) long and was joined by more than 2 million grief-stricken people from Birla House to Yamuna river.

All big Indian cities have a Mahatma Gandhi Road, as do Paris in France, Durban in South Africa, Amsterdam in the Netherlands, and Tehran in Iran.

More than 70 countries have erected statues of Gandhi and released postage stamps honouring him.

US stamp bearing Gandhi's mugshot, 1961

Mapping Gandhi

Mahatma Gandhi continues to be celebrated in many countries in many ways. On his birth centenary in 1969, more than 40 countries, including the UK, released postage stamps to honour Gandhi. His statues dot cities in more than 70 countries. In India, it is hard to miss Gandhi – with his portrait on currency notes and statues in every major city.

PLACES TO VISIT IN INDIA

- National Gandhi Museum and Library, New Delhi
- Kirti Mandir, Porbandar
- Sabarmati Ashram and Museum, Ahmedabad
- Mani Bhavan Gandhi Sangrahalaya, Mumbai
- Magan Sangrahalaya, Wardha
- National Gandhi Memorial Society, Pune
- Gandhi Sangrahalaya, Patna
- Gandhi Bhavan, Thycaud, Trivandrum
- Gandhi Memorial Museum, Madurai
- Gandhi Memorial Museum, Kolkata

Political map of India highlighting places associated with Gandhi

Reluctant Mahatma

It is interesting to imagine how Gandhi would have reacted to the worldwide adulation and honour showered on him. His response to such reverence in his lifetime was one of discomfort: "... I had been afflicted with the title of Mahatma... Often the title has deeply pained me", he said in his autobiography. He once said that he did not feel like a Mahatma and did not understand what a Mahatma was since he had never met one.

USEFUL WEBSITES

www.mkgandhi.org
www.gandhiserve.org
www.navajivantrust.org
www.gandhifoundation.org
www.spiritualmkgandhi.org
www.gandhiashram.org.in
www.gandhiheritageportal.org

World map highlighting countries that have honoured Gandhi

KEY

- ⊙ Museums
- ★ Statues
- ▲ Ashrams
- ⌂ Places where Gandhi stayed
- ● Temples
- ■ Countries that have issued Gandhi stamps

Glossary

Example of the type of portable *charkha* used by Gandhi

ALLIED POWERS Britain, France, and Russia – the countries that fought the Central Powers (Germany, Austria-Hungary, and Turkey) during World War I. These countries were joined by the Soviet Union and USA during World War II in their fight against the Axis Powers, led by Germany, Italy, and Japan.

An illustration featuring the military allies and their flags during World War I

APARTHEID The official system of racial segregation practised in South Africa between 1948 and 1994. Under this system, "blacks" and "coloureds" did not get the same political rights as "whites".

ASHRAM A spiritual retreat, usually away from urban centres, where people dedicate themselves to religious activities and meditation.

ASSASSINATION Murder of a public figure for political, social, or religious reasons.

AXIS POWERS The countries that supported Germany during World War II, chiefly Italy and Japan.

BANIA In Indian society, a person belonging to a caste traditionally involved in trading, moneylending, or shopkeeping.

BRAHMIN One of the four broad social groups, or *varna* – Brahmin, Kshatriya, Vaishya, and Shudra – which make up the traditional Indian caste system. The Brahmins – the highest in the hierarchical caste structure – are priests, scholars, or teachers.

CASTE SYSTEM The traditional Indian system of grouping people as "higher" or "lower" in the social order as per the nature of their work. People were born into their father's caste, did the same work, and married only within their caste.

CHARKHA Hindi for "spinning wheel".

CIVIL DISOBEDIENCE A non-violent form of protest in which the protesters refuse to obey laws that they consider unjust.

COLONY A territory ruled by a foreign country. Also a territory inhabited by a large number of foreigners who go on to dominate its society and politics.

COMMUNIST A person who believes in communism, a political system in which all property is commonly owned by people and all wealth divided among them equally or according to their needs.

Sabarmati Ashram in Ahmedabad, India

DIVIDE AND RULE When a government encourages division between different groups so that they do not remain united to oppose it.

HARIJAN A Hindi word meaning "Children of God". A name given by Mahatma Gandhi to the group of people formerly called "untouchables".

HARTAL A Hindi word for going on strike against a government, employer, or any other authority.

HINDUISM The religion of the majority of people in India, based on a wide range of beliefs and traditions, gods and goddesses, and sacred texts. It evolved over centuries, with no single founder or holy book.

IMPERIALISM The policy of making a country stronger and richer by ruling or exercising control over other countries.

INDENTURED LABOUR A system of servitude, followed between the 19th and 20th centuries, in which indebted persons were bound to employers for a specified time, regardless of harsh conditions or meagre pay.

INDIAN NATIONAL CONGRESS Indian political party that was founded in 1885. It played a key role in the Indian freedom struggle, turning it into a mass movement under the leadership of Mahatma Gandhi.

INDUSTRIAL REVOLUTION The development of machine-made, factory-based, and steam-powered manufacture of goods, which began in 18th-century England and spread across the world. The invention of the steam engine spurred the development of steam boats, railway locomotives, and automobiles.

INNER TEMPLE One of four associations of lawyers (called barristers) and judges in the UK, the other three being Middle Temple, Lincoln's Inn, and Gray's Inn.

ISLAM A religion based on the teachings of Prophet Mohammed, which began in Arabia in the 7th century. Its followers, called Muslims, believe in only one God, Allah, and follow their holy book, the *Quran*.

Quran, the sacred book of Islam

KHILAFAT A political movement in which Muslims protested against the abolishment of the Islamic Caliphate and loss of Caliph's powers after WWI.

KNIGHTHOOD A title given to a man by the British monarch for his achievements or his service to his country.

KSHATRIYA One of the four broad groupings, or *varna*, which make up the traditional Indian caste system. The Kshatriya group includes the ruling and warrior class.

MAHATMA A Sanskrit word for "great soul"; the title given to Mohandas Gandhi to acknowledge his saintly qualities.

NATUROPATHY A system of staying healthy and treating illnesses by natural means such as diet control, massages, and the use of water and sunlight.

Slave chains

PAX BRITANNICA Latin for "British Peace", imposed by the British Empire upon hostile nations in the 19th century.

POORNA SWARAJ A Hindi phrase for "total independence".

PRINCELY STATES The term used by the British rulers for Indian kingdoms.

PROTECTORATE An autonomous territory under the military protection of a stronger country but not directly ruled by it.

RACISM The belief that some people are inferior to others because of their skin colour, leading to prejudice and discrimination against them.

REVOLUTION A thorough change in political, social, or economic systems, taking place over a short period of time.

SATYAGRAHA A Hindi word for "truth-force". Refers to Gandhi's philosophy and strategy of struggling against injustice, using moral force and methods of peaceful civil disobedience.

SCAVENGERS A group of people in India who manually remove human excreta from old-fashioned toilets without flush.

SCHEDULED CASTES The official term used to describe the castes formerly called "untouchables" in India.

SEDITION The political act of inciting people to rebel against a government.

SEPARATE ELECTORATES A system of elections in which people of a certain community vote separately for their own representatives.

SHUDRA One of the four social groups, or *varna*, which make up the traditional Indian caste system. The Shudra group includes manual labourers and is deemed the lowest in the traditional Indian caste hierarchy.

SLAVERY A system in which people were captured and forced to labour, usually without payment, for people who belonged to powerful social groups or nations. Slaves were viewed as the property of their masters.

SOCIALISM A political and economic system in which important economic resources, such as farms and industries, are owned and managed by the government in the name of the public.

SWADESHI A Hindi word for "of own country", referring to products made domestically.

SWARAJ A Hindi word for "self-rule" or "home rule".

SWASTIKA An ancient symbol of good fortune in the Indian subcontinent as well as Europe. A modified version was adopted by Adolf Hitler's Nazi Party as its symbol.

SUFFRAGETTES Female activists who struggled for women's right to vote in the UK and USA, during the late 19th and early 20th centuries.

THEOSOPHISTS A group of spiritualists who explored the origin, nature, and purpose of existence; worked for humanity's spiritual evolution; and were members of the Theosophical Society, a worldwide association founded by Madame Blavatsky and others in 1875.

UNTOUCHABLES People who did work, such as scavenging, considered "impure" in the Indian caste system and fell outside the pale of caste society.

Madame Blavatsky

VAISHNAVA A person belonging to a sect of Hinduism devoted to the worship of Lord Vishnu and his 10 incarnations.

VAISHYA One of the four broad social groups, or *varna*, which make up the Indian caste system. The Vaishya group includes traders and agriculturalists.

VARNA The traditional Indian system of organizing society into four hereditary groups or castes, based on the work people do. The four *varna* are Brahmins (priests and scholars), Kshatriyas (rulers and warriors), Vaishyas (merchants and farmers), and Shudras (menial workers).

WHITE MAN'S BURDEN A 19th-century concept, which said that white Europeans were the most civilized race and as such obliged to teach civilization to inferior races. It was popularized in a Rudyard Kipling poem of the same name.

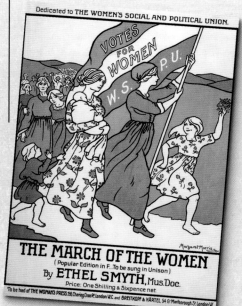

The songsheet of the anthem of the suffragettes, 1911

Index

Acknowledgements

Dorling Kindersley would like to thank: Alka Thakur and Kingshuk Ghoshal for proofreading; Rupa Rao for editorial assistance; Deep Shikha Walia for design assistance; Rakesh Khundongbam for illustrations, and Vikas Kanchan for index.

Special thanks to Dr. Mani Mala and other staff members of Gandhi Smriti and Darshan Samiti for allowing us to use images from their library.

The publisher would like to thank the following for their kind permission to reproduce their photographs:

(Key: a-above; b-below/bottom; c-centre; f-far; l-left; r-right; t-top)

2 Alamy Images: Interfoto (crb); Dinodia Photos (c); Oleksiy Maksymenko (br). Mullock's Auctioneers: (c/prayer beads). Gandhi Smriti and Darshan Samiti: Deepak Aggarwal (bl). Getty Images: British Library / Robana / Hulton Fine Art Collection (cb); Henry Guttmann / Hulton Archive (cl). www.ushaseejarim.com: Usha Seejarim, 2006 (tr). 3 Alamy Images: Interfoto (tl). Gandhi Smriti and Darshan Samiti: Deepak Aggarwal (br). Getty Images: Don Emmert (tr). 4 Corbis: Heritage Images (bl). Dorling Kindersley: Ivy Roy (tr). Dreamstime.com: Fredwellman (tl). Gandhi Smriti and Darshan Samiti: (br); Deepak Aggarwal (c). Getty Images: WIN-Initiative (bc). 5 Gina Rohekar: From the collection of Sherry Rohekar (r). 6 Alamy Images: Oleksiy Maksymenko (cl). 6-7 Corbis: Hulton-Deutsch Collection (b). Getty Images: Imagno / Hulton Archive (c); Mondadori (tr). 8 Alamy Images: The Art Gallery Collection (tl). Dorling Kindersley: Royal Geographical Society, London (cb). 8-9 Dorling Kindersley: The Science Museum, London (b). 9 Corbis: (br). Getty Images: Time & Life Pictures (cr). 10 Alamy Images: Dinodia Photos (r). Gandhi Smriti and Darshan Samiti: (tl). 11 Alamy Images: Dinodia Photos (b). Dorling Kindersley: Romi Chakraborty (br). Gandhi Smriti and Darshan Samiti: (tl). Getty Images: Mondadori (tr). Koshur Saal: Chandramukhi Ganju (cl). 12-13 Corbis: Hulton-Deutsch Collection (b). 12 Getty Images: Henry Guttmann / Hulton Archive (tl). 13 Dorling Kindersley: Ivy Roy (br). Gandhi Smriti and Darshan Samiti: (tl, crb, bc). Getty Images: London Stereoscopic Company / Hulton Archive (tr). 14 Gandhi Smriti and Darshan Samiti: Deepak Aggarwal (cr). Mary Evans Picture Library: Private Collection (c). 14-15 Corbis: Jon Hrusa. 15 Alamy Images: Dinodia Photos (br). Documentation Centre (Ukzn): (tl). Getty Images: Classic Image (bl); Interfoto (tl). The Bridgeman Art Library: Private Collection (c). 16-17 Alamy Images: Dinodia Photos (b). 17 Documentation Centre (Ukzn): (tl/Indian pass, tl/Industrial service, tl/Service contract). Dreamstime.com: Artem Khabeev (tl/hand). Gandhi Smriti and Darshan Samiti: (tr). www.ushaseejarim.com: Usha Seejarim, 2006 (tr). 18 Fotolia: rook76 (bl). 18-19 Corbis: Hulton-Deutsch Collection. 19 akg-images: R. u. S. Michaud (tr). Alamy Images: RGB Ventures LLC dba SuperStock (tr). Corbis: Heritage Images (c). Gandhi Smriti and Darshan Samiti: (cla). Getty Images: David Evans / National Geographic (clb). 20 Alamy Images: North Wind Picture Archives (br). Dreamstime.com: Eyeblink (c/Black pepper). Fotolia: Grecaud Paul (c). Getty Images: British Library / Robana / Hulton Fine Art Collection (tr). 21 Dorling Kindersley: National Railway Museum, New Delhi (br). Getty Images: Hulton Archive (cr); British Library / Robana / Hulton Fine Art Collection (c). Mary Evans Picture Library: (clb). 22 Getty Images: DEA / G. Dagli Orti (cl). 22-23 Gina Rohekar: From the collection of Sherry Rohekar. 23 Gandhi Smriti and Darshan Samiti: (br). Wikipedia: Uma Dhupelia-Mesthrie / Isabell Hofmeyr (cl). 24 Dreamstime.com: Fredwellman (bl). Gandhi Smriti and Darshan Samiti: (tl). 24-25 Alamy Images: Dinodia Photos. 25 Alamy Images: Dinodia Photos (cra); Robert Harding Picture Library Ltd (tl); Seapix (br). Corbis: Rykoff Collection (bl). 26 Alamy Images: Dinodia Photos (br). Getty Images: WIN-Initiative (b). 26-27 Alamy Images: Maurice Joseph (b). Getty Images: Don Emmert (ca). 27 Alamy Images: Dinodia Photos (crb). 28 akg-images: Archiv Peter Rühe (br). Alamy Images: Dinodia Photos (bra). 28-29 Alamy Images: Dinodia Photos. 29 Gandhi Smriti and Darshan Samiti: (tl, c, tr). Getty Images: Wallace Kirkland / TIME & LIFE Images (bl). 30 akg-images: Archiv Peter Rühe (bl). Nehru Memorial Museum & Library: (tl). 30-31 Alamy Images: Dinodia Photos. 31 Alamy Images: Yvan Travert (tr). Corbis: Bettmann (br). The University of Warwick: Iron and Steel Trades Confederation (ISTC), Modern Records Centre (cb). 32 Dreamstime.com: Engin Korkmaz (tl). 32-33 Getty Images: Topical Press Agency / Hulton Archive. 33

Alamy Images: Dinodia Photos (tr). Corbis: Bettmann (br). 34 Alamy Images: Interfoto (tl). 34-35 Getty Images: Rolls Press / Popperfoto. 35 Gandhi Smriti and Darshan Samiti: (tl/Gandhi with charkha). Getty Images: Keren Su / China Span (tl). Manoj Kumar: (tr). 36-37 Alamy Images: Dinodia Photos (t). Corbis: Jim Craigmyle (Background). Dreamstime.com: R. Gino Santa Maria (b/Open book). Gandhi Smriti and Darshan Samiti: Deepak Aggarwal (b). 36 Dreamstime.com: Empire331 (crb); Plmrue (bc); R. Gino Santa Maria (bc/3 books). Getty Images: Universal Images Group (c). 37 Corbis: Bettmann (cb); Hulton-Deutsch Collection (tr). 38 R.K. Laxman: (tl). 38-39 Alamy Images: Dinodia Photos. 39 Gandhi Smriti and Darshan Samiti: (tr). Getty Images: Raveendran / AFP (cr); Margaret Bourke-White / Time & Life Pictures (bl). Vishnu Menon: (br). 40 Alamy Images: Dinodia Photos (b). Corbis: Bettmann (tl). Getty Images: Ivan Vdovin (cla). Corbis: Bettmann (br). Gandhi Smriti and Darshan Samiti: (br). Getty Images: Margaret Bourke-White / Time & Life Pictures (tl); March Of Time / Time & Life Pictures (br). 42 Corbis: Dinodia (cr). 43 akg-images: Archiv Peter Rühe (tl). Alamy Images: Interfoto (cb); Travelib prime (tr); DIZ Muenchen GmbH, Sueddeutsche Zeitung Photo (cl). Getty Images: Mondadori (br/Autographic Letter); Manan Vatsyayana / AFP (br). 44 Alamy Images: Dinodia Photos (b). 45 Corbis: Hulton-Deutsch Collection (tl). Getty Images: UniversalImagesGroup (b). Mary Evans Picture Library: John Frost Newspapers (bc). 46 Getty Images: Keystone-France (l). 46-47 Corbis: Hulton-Deutsch Collection. 47 Alamy Images: PjrStudio (clb). Corbis: CinemaPhoto (cr). 48 Corbis: Heritage Images (bl). 48-49 Corbis: Hulton-Deutsch Collection. 49 Alamy Images: Interfoto (l). Corbis: Bettmann (br). 50 akg-images: Archiv Peter Rühe (clb). Corbis: Hulton-Deutsch Collection (tl). 50-51 Dorling Kindersley: Priyanka Thakur. 51 Corbis: Bettmann (br). 52-53 Getty Images: Keystone-France (b). 52 Getty Images: Popperfoto (cr). 53 Corbis: Hulton-Deutsch Collection (b). Gandhi Smriti and Darshan Samiti: (tr). 54-55 Corbis: Bettmann. 54 Getty Images: Margaret Bourke-White / Time & Life Pictures (tl). 55 Getty Images: Dinodia Photos (br). 56 Getty Images: Keystone / Hulton Archive (r). 56-57 Corbis: Bettmann. Dreamstime.com: Dmitry Rukhlenko (t). 57 Corbis: Raminder Pal Singh / epa (br). Getty Images: Hulton Archive (r). 58-59 Gandhi Smriti and Darshan Samiti. 59 Corbis: Bettmann (bl). Getty Images: Fox Photos / Hulton Archive (r). Nehru Memorial Museum & Library: (bc). 60 Corbis: Radu Sigheti / X00255 / Reuters (cl). 60-61 Corbis: Bettmann. 61 Corbis: Rick Friedman / Pool (br); Pete Marovich (r). Getty Images: Frank Barratt / Hulton Archive (l). 62 Alamy Images: PjrStudio (c). Corbis: Bob Adelman (clb). Getty Images: New York Daily News Archive (tl). 62-63 Corbis: Bettmann. 63 Corbis: Osman Orsal (br). Getty Images: Travel Ink / Gallo Images (cr). 64-65 Corbis: Brandon Tabiolo / Design Pics. 65 Corbis: Hulton-Deutsch Collection (tl); K.J. Historical (bl). Gandhi Smriti and Darshan Samiti: Deepak Aggarwal (br). Getty Images: Science & Society Picture Library (tr). Jamie Tully: (c). 66 Gandhi Smriti and Darshan Samiti: (tl); Deepak Aggarwal (c). Getty Images: NBCUniversal (bl). 66-67 Corbis: Brandon Tabiolo / Design Pics (Background). 67 Alamy Images: Arnel Manalang (r); SCPhotos (tl). 70-71 Corbis: Brandon Tabiolo / Design Pics. 70 Dinudey Baidya: (b). Getty Images: Popperfoto (cl). Gina Rohekar: From the collection of Sherry Rohekar (tc). 71 Corbis: Hulton-Deutsch Collection (tr); Godong / Robert Harding World Imagery (tl); Heritage Images (br). Dorling Kindersley: Royal Geographical Society, London (clb)

Wallchart images: Alamy Images: Interfoto tl, bl/ (boycott of British goods), Dinodia Photos c, tr, PjrStudio cra; The Bridgeman Art Library: Private Collection cla; Corbis: Pete Marovich br, Radu Sigheti / X00255 / Reuters fbr, Raminder Pal Singh / epa crb; Dorling Kindersley: Priyanka Thakur cr; Dreamstime.com: Fredwellman cl; Gandhi Smriti and Darshan Samiti: Deepak Aggarwal cb/ (Hey Ram); Getty Images: David Evans / National Geographic clb, Henry Guttmann / Hulton Archive ftl, WIN-Initiative clb/ (Sandals); R.K. Laxman: bl; Gina Rohekar: cb

Jacket images: Front: Alamy Images: Interfoto c/ (South Africa medal), Oleksiy Maksymenko cl/ (Three monkeys), Dinodia Photos r, cl; Mullock's Auctioneers: c/ (Prayer beads); Dorling Kindersley: Ivy Roy c/ (Sign on the house); Dreamstime.com: Empire331 c/ (Ink and pen), Fredwellman ca / (Charkha); Engin Korkmaz c/ (Ottoman symbol); Gandhi Smriti and Darshan Samiti: Deepak Aggarwal ca, bl/ (Charkha); Getty Images: Don Emmert cb, WIN-Initiative c/ (Wooden sandals); www.ushaseejarim.com: Usha Seejarim, 2006 clb; Back: Gandhi Smriti and Darshan Samiti: l

All other images © Dorling Kindersley
For further information see: www.dkimages.com